Joseph Ellis Coffee Farnham

Providence to Dallas, a Brief Trip to the Southwest

Joseph Ellis Coffee Farnham
Providence to Dallas, a Brief Trip to the Southwest
ISBN/EAN: 9783743350120
Manufactured in Europe, USA, Canada, Australia, Japa
Cover: Foto ©Andreas Hilbeck / pixelio.de

Manufactured and distributed by brebook publishing software (www.brebook.com)

Joseph Ellis Coffee Farnham

Providence to Dallas, a Brief Trip to the Southwest

A Brief Trip to the Southwest

Providence to Dallas

A Brief Trip to the Southwest

BY

J. E. C. FARNHAM

Respectfully Inscribed

TO MY

ASSOCIATE BRETHREN ON THE GRAND BOARD,
PAST AND PRESENT

———

I. O. O. F.

A LIMITED NUMBER OF COPIES
PRINTED FOR
PRIVATE DISTRIBUTION

Preface

PERHAPS it was needless that this book should have been made. The sketch herein narrated was first written for personal pleasure. On reading the first part to the home circle, one of the family said, "Why don't you make a little book of it?" Hence the reason for its appearance.

The account is written connectedly, as if our entire journey was by daylight. The reader, however, comprehending the long distance covered, will at once realize that a large part of it was travelled by night. On the return home, we re-travelled by day certain sections which were traversed in the darkness on the outward trip. Thus were we afforded an opportunity for sight-seeing nearly the entire way. Therefore the story is related unitedly, in order to give a descriptive, connected, and panoramic picture of the country *en-route* from "PROVIDENCE TO DALLAS."

Much of the story related is from observation and from memory; the writer nevertheless acknowledges recourse to different printed works for valuable data and facts woven into the narrative.

J. E. C. F.

May 1, 1897.

Contents

Providence to Niagara Falls.

    Niagara Falls to St. Louis.

        St. Louis to Hot Springs.

            Hot Springs to Dallas.

Providence to Niagara Falls

THE PLEASURE and delight of travel are alike fascinating to him who is so fortunate as to make frequent and long journeys, and to him whose trips are less numerous and more limited. But, aside from the pleasure and delight thus afforded, the educative effect and mental development thereby secured are, to most people, beyond estimate. Charming indeed, in anticipation and in realization, is a trip "across the water" to visit the "mother country," and from thence extending over the eastern continent, and penetrating even into the Oriental lands, rich in ancient biblical lore, and sacred with human and Divine touch of "Him who spake as never man spake," and who, while "manifest in the flesh," "went about doing good."

It is not, however, needful that one should go to the fatherland in order to find delight and pleasure, and to be educated and mentally helped by travel and adventure, for fascinating and helpful to the amplest degree is the charm of mountain and valley, of river and lake, of forest and prairie, of city and country, in our own beautiful, extensive, and loved America.

In visiting different sections, interest and instruction attaches at once and always to the varying customs and manners of the people, to the ever changing variety of the "make-up" of the town or the city, both as to archi-

tectural effect and the dissimilar methods of business
and of trade. While the same general fundamental or
underlying principle governs in the life and business of
our entire American system of States, forming the grand
compact which we are pleased and proud to style the
Federation or National Union, yet in detail the every-
day experiences in the domestic and business career of
our people are essentially different. As varied and as
varying as is the life of our common citizenship, equally
so and more are the variety and change of the country
itself, spread out to view as we spin over the continent
in carriage, stage or car.

A trip in September, 1896, from Providence to the
beautiful southern city of Dallas in the "lone star State,"
afforded me not only intense delight, but also afforded
inestimable mental profit both in the journey to and the
sojourn in the objective city named.

Leaving Providence by the "Consolidated," we joined
our party at Worcester on the Boston and Albany train,
having our own chartered sleeping car through to Chicago. Mutual greetings with friends occasionally seen
were at once exchanged, followed by introductions to
then strangers who immediately became friends, and we
settled down to a social acquaintance which became
almost equal to an endearing family tie, and which continued throughout our four days and nights of travel
together into the "southwest."

The ride through western Massachusetts, amid the
forest-clad Berkshire hills, broken ever and anon by flow-

ing stream and enchanting water-fall, the homes here and there of our frugal and hard-working agriculturalists, the large and busy populated centres, formed, in combination, a picture so winsome as to make lasting impressions upon the memory, and prove a constant delight for future reflection. Continuing on, hour after hour, with ever changing natural panorama, the eye is feasted, while the mind revels in an intellectual treat. Daylight gradually fades, darkness deepens, the panoramic outside picture is lost, the gas is lighted, and we engage in a social evening of conversation and of games. Bed-time arrives, we seek rest in our "sleepers," Morpheus controls our intellect and our powers, and so, day and night on and ever on we roll, stopping only occasionally at a few of the larger stations *en route*. A few brief hours, and the gray tints of morning appear, daylight comes again, we arise from our slumber, which, perchance, has not been as refreshing as repose in our bed at home, yet we feel revived, and after making our toilet, take observations to find where we are, and re-enter upon our pleasurable journey by daylight.

Although ours is a through car, yet we travel by different routes, and, passing from the Boston and Albany to the New York Central and Hudson River railroad, we continue our way across the country of the majestic Empire State, past city and town, mountain and vale, with beautiful level stretches of cultivated land, rich in harvest fruits, the corn ready for the garner, the extensive, numerous and temptings vintages, with luscious and appetizing bunches of grapes hanging in abundance on the vines. At Syracuse our train waits for about twenty-five minutes, and disembarking we enter the graceful railway station, where we partake of a nice breakfast, then resuming our trip fly on to the busy and attractive city of Buffalo, from whence, after a brief tarry, we depart for Niagara Falls, arriving at about noon and in good time for dinner at the Tower House. Here we are to stop for rest and prospecting until evening.

Niagara,—the Indian word for "thunder of the waters," —what a charming spot; who is able to describe it? Much has been written, much will be written, of this wonderful natural attraction, yet its wonders have never been, never can be, fully disclosed. To appreciate Niagara,—this whirling, rolling, tumbling river, with its enchanting falls, its awe-inspiring chasms, its lovely islands, its marvelous springs, its majestic wal ed-in-sides, —this renowned stream, washing the shores of America and of Canada, one must personally visit; and to visit is but to admire and to be enraptured.

It has been said, and right truly, too, "The natural beauty of many falls and cataracts command admiration, but there is only one Niagara." Many are the delights of this romantic spot. For miles amid these interesting surroundings the tourist may wander spell-bound on either hand and all about him. The famous American Fall lies between Prospect Point and Goat Island. It is 1,000 feet across, and millions of gallons of water flow constantly over it to a descent of one hundred and fifty-

GENERAL VIEW OF NIAGARA FALLS FROM PROSPECT POINT.

eight feet; this immense volume of water dashes on the gigantic hidden rocks below, and reacting sends the silvery spray and foam hundreds of feet in the air. It is a magnificent spectacle, a constant delight to the eye, and is so carefully and securely walled about at its extreme edge on the American side that the tourist may stand at its very brink at Prospect Point, with the huge sheet of falling water close to his feet, shielded from harm by an iron balustrade or railing. Above the American Fall the turbulent, swiftly-flowing Niagara river, tossed into perpetual motion, comes tumbling down, the Rapids just above the Fall having a descent of forty feet in half a mile.

The Horseshoe Fall, so named from its horseshoe shape, and sometimes called the Canadian Fall, extends from the side of Goat Island opposite to the American shore across to the Dominion of Canada. The fall of the water here is equally picturesque, and has about the same descent as the American Fall. It is estimated that 15,000,000 cubic feet of water pass over the Falls every minute, or about one cubic mile per week. Above the Horseshoe Fall are the Cascade Rapids, having a seething rolling descent of nearly fifty-five feet in three quarters of a mile. The great chain of lakes above the Falls, supplied by the streams from the valleys, the rains and the melting snows from the mountains, are ever feeding and never cease in their supply of this vast volume of water,— so grand, so awful, so sublime, so magnificent, so fascinating, in its varied flow and fall over these colossal chasms and hidden rocks, on and ever on, out through

HORSESHOE FALL FROM GOAT ISLAND.

the neighborly lake, the contiguous streams, rivers and water-ways, until it loses itself in the great ocean. The entire system is a stately problem of nature, unsolved and unsolvable, nevertheless man, with his genius, his science and his mathematics, has been for ages working at this problem, and many interesting facts of this marvelous, unrivaled stream, have been adduced.

Many are the points of interest in and about Niagara. So numerous are they that to detail them would be to write a book of many pages; a brief mention of some of these, however, will be of interest.

Prospect Park is a State reservation, containing twelve acres, with an extended frontage on the gorge and on the river just above the American Fall. Here stands the Library Building, where one may "examine charts of all the great lakes and the source of the water down the Niagara and St. Lawrence rivers."

From Goat Island Bridge one of the finest of the many attractive views of Niagara is afforded. As you stand here you may discover, at your left, Brig Island and Ship Island, while at your right you may behold Avery's Rocks, Chapin Island, Robinson Island, Blackbird Island, and Crow Island, to which "there is no access as it is felt that they are far more attractive in appearance than they would be bridged. Lovers of natural scenery, who admire the perfection of these green islands removed from the touch of man, will rejoice to see them remain in their present isolated condition, illustrations of the beauty and harmony of nature's handiwork."

Passing on we come to "Bath Island, so named from the fact that years ago there were bath-houses located there." On this island is the office of the Commissioners of the State Reservation at Niagara.

Still passing on, across another bridge, and we come to Goat Island with its adjacent smaller islands, which together embrace about eighty acres. This island obtained the name which it bears from the fact "that, in 1779, John Steadman having cleared a portion of the upper end, placed some goats upon it, and afterwards neglected to care for them. The coldness of the ensuing winter killed them," and thus arose the name Goat Island. This spot " is to-day a temple of nature, at whose shrine thousands of people from all over the world annually pay their tribute of praise." It is, indeed, sacred ground from the lavishness of nature in the sublimity of its attractions.

Picturesque " Luna Island is reached by a substantial stairway and bridge which spans a graceful sheet of water sixty feet wide. The island derives its name from the fact that the Lunar bow is seen here to the best advantage." " The island trembles from the fearful force of the falling water. It was while standing here, on Sunday, October 13, 1889, that a member of the Pan-American party observed that it was standing as near death as possible. The view here is a very desirable one, and especially is this true while standing at the top of the stairway leading to the island. The American Fall is seen in all of its magnificence, and the eye follows the gorge for fully two miles." Between Luna Island and Goat Island is a pretty water-fall called the Central Fall.

From Goat Island, on its westerly side, are the Biddle Stairs, which were built in 1829, to enable visitors to descend to the Cave of the Winds. A visit to this wonderful Cave necessitates the donning of a water-proof dress, and it is essential, too, that one has an experienced guide, as such a visit is not unattended with danger. " Standing in the Cave the beautiful sheet of water falls before you, and the outer world is curtained from view." This remarkable Cave is a sublime sight, and has been "formed wholly by the action of the water washing away the soft substratum of the precipice, and the hard limestone rock is left arching above."

At the top of the cliff, after proceeding a little further in the midst of the beautiful surroundings Terrapin Point is reached. From here, standing right at the edge of the Fall, just where it pours over the precipice, one has a grand view. "A more imposing sight cannot be imagined. In the gorge below, the Niagara continues toward Lake Ontario, boiling and seething, after the plunge, and for fully 1,000 feet from the base of the Falls is as white as milk. Above are the Rapids, rushing towards you, and it is in the midst of such surroundings that the weakness of man is most apparent."

A charm amid this charming locality is the Three Sister Islands. From here you have an unsurpassed view of the Canadian Rapids, which run at the rate of twenty-eight miles per hour. Here before you are the beautiful

Upper Rapids, and the spot is truly entrancing. Pass from one to the other of these islands, and from each the view is admirable. "From the head of the Third Sister Island may be seen one continuous cascade, extending from Goat Island to the Canadian shore, varying from ten to twenty feet in height. But a short distance along this line of breakers is Spouting Rock, so named from its frequent tossing of the water high in the air."

Returning to the head of Goat Island, reached by following the road to the east, we obtain a fine view of the upper portion of Niagara river, which is broad, quiet, and placid, failing in the slightest degree to convey the announcement of the fearful rough waters below. Rambling about the island, before crossing the bridges to return to the mainland, the tourist will find captivating scenes innumerable to hold him in admiration and in awe.

To derive the most possible from a visit to Niagara, and to make sure that none of the almost countless beauties and attractions are passed by unnoticed and unknown, it is not only desirable but absolutely needful that you provide yourself with an experienced guide and a convenient conveyance.

To meet the requirements of visitors of moderate means, and afford to them an opportunity for sight seeing at a small cost, there has been constructed and is now in successful operation on the American side of the river an electric railway, called The Great Gorge Route, running from the city of Niagara Falls to Lewiston, a distance of seven miles. This ride, for natural scenery, grandeur, and constant absorbing interest, is unexcelled by any similar stretch of railroad in the world. Journeying by this road, which is equipped with as fine electric cars as have ever been built, we are soon at the river, and as we travel down through the gorge, closely following the river's side, every moment is one of pleasure with its ever dissolving and entertaining views. Prominent of these is The Whirlpool Rapids, about two miles below the Falls. Here

PASSING WHIRLPOOL RAPIDS, AMERICAN SIDE
THE GREAT GORGE ROUTE

"the quiet surface of the river is broken as the waters plunge in their maddening course to the lower lake through the narrow gorge only three hundred feet wide." Lashed and tumbled into a milky whiteness, the terrific force of this ponderous mass of water would produce vast havoc but for the formidable banks on either side which hold it in supreme check. These Rapids, in all their beauty and majesty, can be viewed and admired in perfect safety while standing at the very river's edge. Elevators have been constructed, on both the American and Canadian sides of the river, by which the tourist may descend about three hundred feet and thus more closely gaze upon this lovely and sublime sight. In these Rapids the water eddys and circles with immense whirling force, and it is so tenacious in its grasp that various objects, dead bodies of men and of animals, who have unfortunately become victims to its embrace, are held for days and even for weeks almost in a given spot without passing further down the river.

A conspicuous object witnessed on our ride through the gorge is the famous Brock's Monument, located at Queenston Heights, on the Canadian side, seven miles below the Falls. This is a handsome and imposing shaft, "erected to perpetuate the memory of General Isaac Brock, who fell here in 1813." In 1826 the first monument was built, was one hundred and twenty-six feet high, and on the night of April 17, 1840, was destroyed by an explosion. This "was replaced by the present structure in 1853. It is one hundred and eighty-five feet in height, the base being forty feet square and thirty feet high." It is exceedingly grand in its mechanism, and is surmounted by a statute of General Brock. A spiral staircase of two hundred and fifty steps, starting from the interior of the base, enables visitors to reach its summit.

GIANT ROCK ON THE GREAT GORGE ROUTE

At various points on our ride, as we make numerous bends and turns in the road, looking up through the gorge at this ever interesting river, nothing but enchantment and delight greets the eye.

We arrive at length at Lewiston, an historic village

nestling beneath the mountain. It derives its name from, and thus perpetually memorializes, Governor Lewis of New York. As far as Lewiston the Niagara river is navigable, and the boats of the Niagara Steam Navigation Company ply between here and Toronto. On our arrival at Lewiston, we have reached the end of this new but famous electric road, and the trolley is reversed for the return trip. Previous to the start, however, "our party" take positions at the ends of the seats and on the side foot-boards of the car, and our picture is taken by our attendant photographer. Again we are off, returning by the same route by which we came, and review the picturesque panorama of the trip down with as much satisfaction as we at first beheld it.

Joy and wonder never cease at this famous locality, and the eye does not weary of repeated visions of these superior natural pictures, but on the contrary is constantly feasted and gladdened,

On the Canadian side of the river there are many, very many, equally enchanting wonders and delights, but space forbids narration.

Added to what nature has so richly provided at this renowned resort, a visitor would be blind indeed, and basely ungrateful, did he not notice and admire what the genius and mechanical skill of man has also placed here for his use and for his appreciation. Notable amid the attractions of Niagara are the massive bridges spanning the river, uniting not only the two opposite shores, but also uniting two important nations, each of whom are

proud in all that Niagara affords, whether it be awe-inspiring natural phenomena or the outcome of the ingenuity of the human brain. Engineering skill is here demonstrated to almost if not quite the acme of human perfection. No grander or more sublime locality can anywhere be found, so rich in its facilities for setting forth man's talents and giving to his inventive intellect full and unlimited sway, than is afforded by this marvellous gorge through which flows this magnetic and restless river. Hung high in mid-air, stretching across emptiness, these majestic bridges convey, in perfect safety, pedestrians, carriages, and railroad trains from one shore to the other. One writer has well said, referring to the three noted bridges spanning this river, "Even if the Falls did not exist as a greater attraction, these bridges would be worth a journey of many miles to see."

The New Suspension Bridge, so stately and grand in its construction, was built "to replace the bridge blown down by the great wind storm of January 10, 1889." The bridge destroyed was comparatively a new one, was 1,268 feet long, was of immense weight, and of apparent great strength. So severe was the storm which demolished this bridge, that its destruction was total, and its splendid proportions and solidity yielded completely to the force of the gale. From each of the towers, on either side of the river, the immense cables were severed with the cleanness of cut of some sharp instrument deftly employed, and the bridge of beauty and of utility was swept into the raging torrent below. Projecting beyond either of the opposite cliffs not an inch of the bridge remained, and the great mass of it lies to-day hidden from sight far below the deep and swiftly-flowing river. Only the bridge proper was destroyed, the huge cables and stately towers remain-

ALONG NIAGARA'S LOWER RAPIDS
THE GREAT GORGE ROUTE

ing intact. The storm which swept away this bridge was one of the fiercest yet known, the wind was from the southwest, and so loud and terrific was the gale, combined with the roar of the angry waters, that the gate-keeper in the office within twenty feet of the end of the bridge did not know until daylight that the structure had fallen. On March 22, 1889, the present new, graceful, and substantial bridge was commenced, and, amazing as it may appear, it was finished on the 7th of the following May. Its length is the same as its predecessor,— 1,268 feet. On the American side the tower is ninety-seven feet and six inches in height; the one on the Canadian side one hundred and three feet and seven inches. Variation in the opposite banks of the river accounts for the difference in the height of these towers. "The width of the structure is seventeen feet six inches between the centres of chords. The weight of the bridge is three hundred and nineteen tons. It is suspended from four cables, each of which is six and one-half inches in diameter, and formed by seven wire ropes, whose diameter is two and one-fourth inches, and in each of which there are one hundred and thirty-three wires. Each of these seven is capable of sustaining one hundred and fifty-five tons, thereby making the sustaining power twenty-eight times one hundred and fifty-five tons," $= 4,340$ tons. From this description some conception may be had of the immensity of this excellent bridge, in its strength and in its completeness of construction. It is located furthest up the river, near the Falls, and is adapted to the use of pedestrians and carriages.

Two miles from the Falls, down the river, near the Whirlpool Rapids, is the Railway Suspension Bridge. This, too, is an equally imposing and impressive structure. Over it pass the trains of the Grand Trunk Railroad and of the Erie Railroad. A stock company owns and controls this " noble viaduct." In 1852 it was commenced, and it was not until March 8, 1855, that the first train passed over it. The present bridge is constructed wholly of steel, displacing the original bridge here built, which was of

PASSING DEVIL'S HOLE RAPIDS
THE GREAT GORGE ROUTE

wood with shore towers of stone. The construction of this bridge is adapted not only to railroad trains but also to carriages and pedestrians, the carriage way being twenty-eight feet below the railroad bed. The length of the span is eight hundred and twenty-five feet from centre to centre of the towers,— the tower on the American

THE CANTALIVER BRIDGE
MICHIGAN CENTRAL RAILROAD

side being eighty-eight feet high, and the opposite on the Canadian side being seventy-eight feet. There are 3,659 tons of No. 9 wire in each cable, and the ultimate aggregate strength of cables is 12,400 tons. The weight of the superstructure is eight hundred tons, and the maximum weight which it will support is 7,309 tons.

Just south of this bridge, and making a close neighbor to it, and situated between it and the new Suspension Bridge, is the celebrated Cantaliver Bridge, over which pass the trains of the Michigan Central Railroad. Work on this bridge was begun April 15, 1883, and it was finished December 1st of the same year. Upon the approach of a train to this bridge gates are opened by an attendant, which are immediately closed as soon as the train has passed. Magnificent in its proportions, grand in its architecture, apparently faultless in its build, it is a joy and a marvel to gaze upon. Its mechanism has, by another, been well described, and it is worthy of repetition here : " Each end is made up of a section, entirely of steel, extending from the shore nearly half way over the chasm. Each section is supported near its centre by a strong steel tower, from which extend two lever arms, one reaching the rocky bluffs, the other extending over the river one hundred and seventy-five feet beyond the towers. The outer arms having no support, and being subject like the other to the weight of trains, a counter-advantage is given by the shore arm being firmly anchored to the rocks on the shore. The towers on either side rise from the water's edge; between them a clear span of four hundred and ninety-five feet over the river, the longest double-track truss-span in the world. The ends of the cantalivers reaching on each side three hundred and ninety-five feet from the abutments, leave a gap of one hundred and twenty feet, filled by an ordinary truss bridge hung from the ends of the cantalivers. Here provision is made for expansion and contraction by an ingenious arrangement between the ends of the truss bridge and of the cantalivers, allowing the ends to move freely as the temperature changes, but at the same time preserving perfect rigidity against side pressure from the wind. There are no guys for this purpose, as in a suspension bridge, but the structure is complete within itself. The total length of the bridge is nine hundred and ten feet. It has a double track, and is strong enough to carry upon each track at the same time the heaviest freight train, extending the entire length of the bridge, headed by two 'consolidation' engines and under a side pressure of thirty pounds per square foot, produced by a wind having a velocity of seventy-five miles per hour, and even then will be strained to only one-fifth of its ultimate strength." While this bridge materially varies in construction from the two suspension bridges noted, yet, like them, it is "suspended," in so far as it is fastened or anchored only to the firm earth and rock of each shore.

To value these bridges for what they really are, in their beauty, their majesty, their symmetry, their strength, and their vast utility, one must fully comprehend the fact that there can be no support for either of them only as it is had from a hold on *terra-firma* from each opposite bank of the river. They are, indeed, each and all of them, marvels of man's intellect, his genius, his architecture, his engineering skill, and his mechanical finish.

In addition to spanning this river with these useful thoroughfares, man, with his practical and utilitarian brain, has for years been endeavoring to harness the immense powers of this Niagara cataract to some useful purpose, and recently very determined success has been the result. Notwithstanding tremendous engineering and mechanical difficulties, the hitherto "waste of waters" of Niagara are now doing valiant and useful service. The Niagara Falls Power Company are the successful promoters of this gigantic enterprise, and the street cars of Buffalo, and the electric lights, too, are run by an insignificant fraction of the force of the tumbling, falling waters of Niagara upwards of twenty miles away. Yet the hydraulic canal is the largest ever constructed, and each one of the giant turbines and dynamos turns 5,000 horsepower into electrical force.

But the day is gone, we cannot linger longer amid the magic spell of the one and only Niagara. We must, reluctantly as we may, quit these scenes, and continue on our way. Consequently we re-enter our "Wagner," and again start away by the Michigan Central in pursuance of our journey to the southwest.

Niagara Falls to St. Louis

EAVING the American side of Niagara Falls, we are taken across the enchanting Niagara river, via the stately Cantaliver bridge, into the Ontario province of Canada. Glancing downward from the car window we have a new view of the river, the seething waters of which are sublimely grand from our elevated position over them. As we pass from the bridge we are mentally reminded that we are now in another domain. Leaving Niagara Falls in New York we enter Clifton upon coming into Canada, and passing on to the next station, a little more than a mile distant, we are at Niagara Falls, Canada, as the inhabitants on each side of the river near the Falls have chosen to give to their settlement the same designation.

Prior to crossing the river and entering Canada a government official of the dominion satisfies himself that everything is all right, that there is "no smuggling," and after inspecting the baggage car, he secures and carefully guards it until we again reach the American shore in Michigan. The third station at which we stop after entering upon the Queen's territory is Falls View. This is vantage ground, indeed, for an extended sight of both the American and Horseshoe Falls, as also for a far-reaching glance down the river below the Falls through the gorge, furnishing a charming view of the restless Rapids. At

RAPIDS FROM CANTALIVER BRIDGE.

this station, along the river's side, a fine level walk-way of flagging, protected by an iron railing or balustrade, has been provided by the Michigan Central Railroad. The trains of this company, passing in either direction, here remain five minutes, extending to passengers the privilege of stepping from the cars to the river's brink to witness and to enjoy the delightful scene,— a privilege

TRAIN AT FALLS VIEW, ONTARIO.
MICHIGAN CENTRAL RAILROAD.

that is justly appreciated and fully improved. The entire limit of time thus allotted is wholly occupied, passengers reluctantly leaving the spot to return to the train.

Our journey across Canada covers about two hundred and twenty-six miles, traversing near its southern boundary, bordering on Lake Erie. Did we not know that we were upon territory of another government we should hardly realize the fact, as there is nothing special to indicate to us that it is other than a part of our own Republic. It is American surely, and many share the opinion that it properly belongs to the United States. Nevertheless this vast country on the north, like the Republic of Mexico on the south, is with us but not of us. Our ride in Canada takes us largely through the farming sections, and the land under tillage as indeed the grass and pasture lots indicate good soil. The country on the line of our journey is rather sparsely settled, and the homes of the inhabitants are not specially attractive. While there are indications of thrift and industry on either hand, and evidences of frugality and economy, yet it is clearly apparent that the people are not dominated by the restless rush and persistent activity of the average American.

St. Thomas is the largest of the Canadian stations on our way, and briefly tarrying at the railway restaurant for a lunch, we are convinced, by a practical test, that sweet milk, good eggs, prime coffee and choice fruits are not unknown here. In addition, too, we found that they were adepts in their preparation of sandwiches, as indeed in all their lines of cookery they were highly efficient. Our palatable repast over, we re-entered our car, and departed with physical satisfaction and with mental gratitude to our Canadian cousins for the excellence of the viands furnished us.

The dining car service of the Michigan Central Railway is most popular with its patrons. Nothing is lacking in the service to render it less than first-class in every respect. The buffet cars are simply palatial, and the management and attendants are actively alert in catering to the wants of the traveller. It has no superior, if an equal.

Some of the more important cities and towns in Canada through which we pass are Welland, Hagersville,

MICHIGAN CENTRAL STATION, ESSEX, ONTARIO.

Waterford, St. Thomas, St. Clair Junction, Comber, Essex, and Windsor. At these several localities substantial and convenient railway depots or stations have been provided, yet the not very close observer will at once discover that the architectual effect, attractive appearance, and ample conveniences of the average city railway station of the United States are not as greatly in evidence in Canada.

Clear skies, bright sunshine, and a moderate temperature, are attendant with us as we travel,— these best of weather conditions furnishing to us all that could be desired for the fullest enjoyment of the constantly changing lanscape scenery. The mountain and valley, and the picturesque rolling land of New England and of the Empire State, are in striking contrast with this Canadian

TRANSFER STEAMER, DETROIT, MICHIGAN.
MICHIGAN CENTRAL RAILROAD.

territory through which we pass, which is remarkably level and dry. This is also notably true throughout the middle western states, prairie land abounding and stretch- for miles in either direction.

Our trip in Canada terminates at Windsor. Here we are confronted by the Detroit river, about a mile in width, which flows between Canada and the State of Michigan.

To continue on our way we must pass this barrier. This is successfully acccomplished by means of an immense ferry-boat. Our lengthy train, made up mostly of "sleepers," is broken into three sections, placed on board of the boat and firmly secured. Thus we are ferried over to the American shore. The trip across this river is most interesting. Steam and sailing craft, plying in either direction, are numerous, while the shores on both sides, representing as they do the two foremost nations of the world, as well as the rippling, sparkling water of the river, charm and hold the eye with constant delight.

From the ferry we are landed at Detroit, Michigan. This is the chief city of the State, is beautiful in its layout, and highly important for its commerce and for its manufactures and other industries. By the last census Detroit had a population of 205,667, averaging of native and foreign born, blacks and whites, about equal with the ordinary northern American cities. The railway station here is imposing, is commodious and convenient, and in the long train sheds attached there is constant activity with arriving and departing trains. Eight lines of railroad enter Detroit, radiating to all important centres, thus adding materially to its business and general interests.

Detroit is located on the river of the same name, and although a number of miles from a lake on either side of it, yet it may very properly be called a lakeport, and one of the most, if not the most, important commercial ports of the northern middle section of our country. Indeed, it is claimed for Detroit that it has the best harbor on either of the great lakes or their tributaries, and is therefore a commercial city of rare advantage. Official statistics show that very few ocean ports exceed the tonnage of its commerce.

DETROIT STATION, SHOWING TRAIN SHEDS.
MICHIGAN CENTRAL RAILROAD.

The Detroit river, which forms the marginal line of the city on the southwest, connects Lake St. Clair with Lake Erie, and is twenty-two miles long, and from one-half a mile to three miles in width.

Detroit is seven miles from Lake St. Clair and eighteen

depots, warehouses, and sundry other industries of varying magnitude.

Situated on slightly rolling land, that section on which the principal part of the city stands rises gradually from the river to a height of from twenty to thirty feet, and then sinking, again rises to a height of forty to fifty feet above the river.

The industrial interests of Detroit are many. A large foreign trade is conducted with Canada, while the exports and imports in numerous other commercial enterprises are vast. Local manufactures, many of large capacity, furnish employment for multitudes of both sexes. Lumber, flour, grain, apples and other fruits, as also a variety of other products constitute a good part of the trade of this busy city, and in addition there are extensive dealings in cattle and hogs. The iron industry is specially prominent, immense quantities of iron ore from the Lake Superior iron regions being here converted into a multiplicity of articles for every-day use. Here, too, are rolling mills, car factories, and many other manufacturing establishments, of differing degrees of importance, which are unrivalled in the amount of their output and in the quality of their products.

Detroit is attractive in its layout, although, perhaps, a little irregular in its completeness. In the design of its streets, two plans have been used,— one radiating from the Grand Circus, and the other with streets running at right angles. The avenues are generally wide, differing in width from one hundred to two hundred feet, and the

WOODWARD AVENUE, DETROIT, MICHIGAN.

streets while narrower yet have a good width, varying from fifty to one hundred feet.

The park system of the city is one of its essential features, the Grand Circus, semi-circular in shape, being the principal park of the city. The architectural effect of the city is admirable, many handsome buildings adorning the streets and avenues, and notable of these are the churches, several of which are effectively grand in finish.

CITY HALL, DETROIT.

A City Hall, pretentious, ornate, substantial and pleasing, is the most prominent of the public buildings. It is two hundred feet long, ninety feet wide, sixty-six feet high to the cornice, one hundred and eighty feet to the top of the tower, and was completed in 1871 at an expense of $600,000. It is built of sandstone, in the Italian style, and is three stories above the basement.

Altogether, Detroit is a magnificent American city, and

we would like to linger here but must forbear and continue on our way.

From Detroit we travel nearly two hundred and twenty-five miles across the southern section of the peninsula State of Michigan, the country on either side commanding our attention and appreciation. The cities and towns through which we pass evidence a tasty and progressive citizenship, and are " up-to-date " in enterprise and appearance. Principal of these is Wayne, Ypsilanti,

RESIDENCE OF GEN. RUSSELL A. ALGER,
DETROIT, MICHIGAN.

Ann Arbor, Jackson, Battle Creek, Kalamazoo, New Buffalo, and Niles. Ann Arbor is familiarly famous as the seat of the noted Michigan State University, which is one of the most influential and helpful of our excellent American colleges.

In a modest and unobtrusive manner the Michigan Central company began, some time ago, to distribute to the women and children passengers on their trains the surplus flowers from the plants which are raised to beau-

CAMPUS, UNIVERSITY OF MICHIGAN, ANN ARBOR.

tify the grounds about the several stations *en route.* So highly prized was this courtesy, that the simple original act has developed into a regular custom, which has indeed become famous. From the extensive conservatories of the company at Ypsilanti and Niles, Michigan, nearly or quite 100,000 bouquets and boutonnieres are thus yearly

DISTRIBUTION OF FLOWERS IN MICHIGAN CENTRAL COACHES.

distributed. This is a practice most liberal, and one which is highly prized by the lady and children passengers, and is also one which is thoroughly appreciated by their male attendants.

Leaving the State of Michigan we make a short cut across the northwestern corner of Indiana, and entering

Illinois terminate this part of our trip by the Michigan Central Railroad in the elegant Central station at Chicago.

Entering Chicago by train, we are delighted with its beautiful suburban annexations, and we pass through the annexed city of Pullman, famous from the name of the "Pullman sleeper," from which industry this pretty set-

MICHIGAN CENTRAL STATION, NILES.

tlement has sprung, and which locality is justly noted for the cleanness of its politics, and for the pure and peaceful habits of its people,— temperance and good morals being healthfully leading. Continuing on, we pass in close sight of Jackson Park, the spot on which the Magic

White City, or World's Fair of 1893, was located; then still on through the Hyde Park district, another of Chicago's beautiful suburban annexes, which is also noted for its temperance and moral atmosphere, its fine residences, and its broad, regular avenues; and still further continue

MICHIGAN CENTRAL STATION, CHICAGO
FRONT VIEW.

on, all the while in the city, for some six or eight miles, along the margin of the vast Lake Michigan to the Central station of the Michigan Central and the Illinois Central Railroads, near the centre of the city. It is needless to say that this station, in its architecture, its completeness, its conveniences, its size, and its various appointments, ranks with the best in the United States.

An involuntary spirit of sadness possessed us as we rode by Jackson Park. This spot, so enchantingly admirable, every part of which was a delight to the eye and a feast to the mind, alive and active to the superlative

INTERIOR CHICAGO STATION.
MICHIGAN CENTRAL RAILROAD.

degree, with its thousands upon thousands of visitors from every civilized sphere, when it was used for and bore the proud distinction of the peerless World's Fair of 1893, was now, as we rode by it, a barren and desolate waste. Hardly a trace remained of its former loveliness, glory and prestige, as the then pride of the entire world. Stony-island avenue, running by the front of this park,

MICHIGAN CENTRAL STATION, CHICAGO.
END VIEW.

said we, great are the vicissitudes of life, marvellous indeed are its kaleidoscopic experiences, and depressing almost to despair are many of its unceasing changes.

Everybody knows of this renowned, energetic and rapidly growing so-called "windy city." As just stated, only so recent as 1893 pilgrimages were made, not alone from every part of our own land, but from all over the world, to attend the far-famed World's Fair held here from May to November of that year. This immense city, situated on the east shore of Lake Michigan, is the great commercial metropolis of the northwest. It is the second largest city in the United States, has a population of 1,098,576, in which foreign born inhabitants are decidedly in the majority, and it thus has a bearing and an effect upon the diversified interests of our great Republic which are far more than ordinarily significant. The streets, avenues and boulevards of Chicago, collectively at least, are the finest, most attractive and beautiful to be found in the world, as to width and convenience, and the residences and business blocks on either side are of stately and solid character.

In public parks this city is unexcelled. Of these, Lincoln Park, of two hundred and fifty acres, magnificent in its avenues, its lawns, its flower beds, its memorial statues, and almost innumerable other attractions, its seventy miles or thereabouts of hard, level driveways, is pre-eminent amid the parks of the world. Prominent of the famous statues of this park are "The Lincoln," memorializing the loved and martyred president and great emancipator, the gift of Eli Bates; and "The Grant Monument," memorializing the peerless soldier, statesman, and president. Besides this park, Humbolt, Garfield, Douglas, and Washington Parks, are simply localities of splendor, exquisite in all their plan and layout, nothing being lacking for beauty and adornment which money can procure. In Washington Park the floral display is nothing less than a work of art, ingenious and elaborate, wrought in designs unique and elegant, and in this respect this park is hardly equalled by any other in the world. While Lincoln Park is the larger of these famous parks, yet the others mentioned are prodigous, each containing about two hundred acres. It matters not how remotely separated these parks may be from each other, twenty miles intervening in some instances, yet the entire system is connected by wide, level, hard, and smooth-as-a-floor boulevards, from which all traffic teams are excluded. On these may be seen throughout the bright days equipages exquisite, resplendent in their shining livery, and exhibiting a grade of carriage and saddle horses such as are rarely seen.

For a number of years, in our large metropolitan centres, the tendency has been in modern architecture to build "into the heavens." As a result it is not uncommon to see in the larger cities buisness blocks, almost faultless in architecture, towering aloft from ten to more than twenty stories. In this respect Chicago leads the world, no other city having so large and compact a number of "sky-scrapers." In 1882, the first of these tall buildings was erected, "The Montauk," on Monroe street, which attains to a height of one hundred and thirty feet, in ten stories, being then the pride and admiration of the city.

Numerous, indeed, have been the erection of these

since then. Notable and the most prominent of them all is The Masonic Temple. While in the hands of the builders its progress was watched with absorbing interest. In its construction was a solution of the question, " How high up must we build on a piece of land worth a million

MASONIC TEMPLE, CHICAGO.

and a half in order to pay rent, interest on capital invested, and running expenses, and also make a profit." Its exterior is imposing, not especially ornamental, yet is magnetically attractive. Entering its forty-foot arch, our attention is drawn to its columns, which are probably the largest in America, we look upward, and three hundred and two feet above is the skylight. Fourteen passenger and two freight elevators fill the rear semi-circle of the rotunda. The top story is a large observatory, and as many as 72,000 people on a single day have been taken by these elevators to this charming lookout. This observatory, which is the chief interior feature of this immense building, will accommodate about 2,000 persons at a time. Located on the twenty-first story, occupying the entire floor, it has sides of heavy glass, which may be entirely removed in good weather. The prospect from this site is beyond description. Spread out to view for miles in either direction, the picture furnished by nature affords not only delight to the eye, but more forcibly provides material for mental reflection which is inexhaustible. The broad silvery waters of Lake Michigan, stretching away into emptiness; the extensive lengths of the compact, solid and massive city, radiating from every point of the compass, and on for miles beyond over the flat broad stretch of country, all in attractive combination, forms a paonrama of unsurpassed natural beauty. In winter this room is heated, sight-seers flock here by the thousands, and from its windows exquisite views of crystalline, in snow and ice, enrapt and charm the eye. To add to the attractiveness of this resort, entertainments of variety and merit are given throughout the fall and winter months. The elevators which take us to this great altitude move quickly, and " it is necessary that passengers should stand quietly, leaning against the side of the car if they feel the need of support." From the first floor to the skylight this mammoth building is a hollow square. Stores and shops occupy the first ten floors; the succeeding six are used for offices; the seventeenth, eighteenth, nineteenth and twentieth are dedicated to masonic uses, representing the various branches of masonry, with ample and convenient accessories of rooms for committees, paraphernalia, banquet halls, etc. Hot and cold water, gas and electric lighting are supplied to every room, in addition to all other so-called modern conveniences. Rows of electric lights about the summit of this building give to its exterior by night a pleasing and effective appearance. It is estimated that up and down to the various lines of business in this building 100,000 persons pass daily. This Masonic Temple, standing matchless amid the famous buildings of our country, is a marvel of genius and skill, was begun in November 1890, completed in the summer of 1892, and cost $3,500,000. It is owned and controlled by a joint stock company of Free Masons.

The mercantile section of Chicago is unrivalled in the substantial character, height and architectural beauty of its business blocks and warehouses. This fact impressively signalizes the extent and volume of trade of this large and influential city. A prominent business here is the slaughter of beeves, hogs and sheep, this city being a centre for almost the entire world in supplying dressed meats for domestic use. The stock-yards, so called, embrace some of the largest firms or corporations, measured from invested capital, anywhere to be found in the business of the world. They are, too, essentially a business most exclusive and independent. Every accessory necessary to the conduct of trade, including their own corporation stores, hotel, bank, etc., are connected with this gigantic industry. At the George B. Swift yards, alone, 5,000 head of cattle, on the average, are daily slaughtered, as also hogs and sheep to the number of several thousand. The fact that from this one house the trade with the local markets of the city amounts to about one hundred thousand dollars per week indicates the immesity of this business, which is forcefully emphasized in reflection upon the large shipments of dressed meats from here to the cities and towns of the United States and to foreign ports.

In wealth, material progress, business push, and constant advance, Chicago has, for a nnmber of years, attracted and held the undivided attention of the civilized world, and this fact has produced, moderately at least, an enviable jealousy on the part of rival cities.

Our trip from Chicago is by the Illinois Central Railroad, on its fast vestibule train the "Daylight Special," starting about half past ten in the morning, after a good breakfast, direct for St. Louis, arriving there in the early evening, the weather throughout the day being all that could be desired for comfortable travelling. Pleasureable in the extreme was this all-day ride, our coaches riding easily, and being seated with chairs materially added to individual comfort. Between these two cities our journey was almost entirely within the State of Illinois, the country on either side and all about us being flat, dry prairie land. Journeying south and southwest, we traverse nearly the entire length of the State, reaching the border on the southwest. Dividing and flowing between the States of Illinois and Missouri is the noted Mississippi river. Crossing this river by the famous Eads bridge, we enter East St. Louis, and pass on to the city of St. Louis.

"DAYLIGHT SPECIAL."
ILLINOIS CENTRAL RAILROAD.

Debris, wreckage, and several of the buildings retopped and repaired reminded us, as we passed through East St. Louis and entered St. Louis, of the serious havoc wrought by the terrific cyclone which occurred on May 27th previous to our visit.

St. Louis is another of those progressive, mercantile and social centres which has given to our southwest character and position amid the populous marts of the United

States. It is the great metropolis of the Mississippi valley, and it is more than an average example of the thrift, industry, prudence and economy of this ever-advancing Republic, and of the determination, hustle and success of the American people.

The Union railway station, where our trip by the Illinois Central railroad ends, is the largest, handsomest, most convenient, stately, and beautiful railway passenger

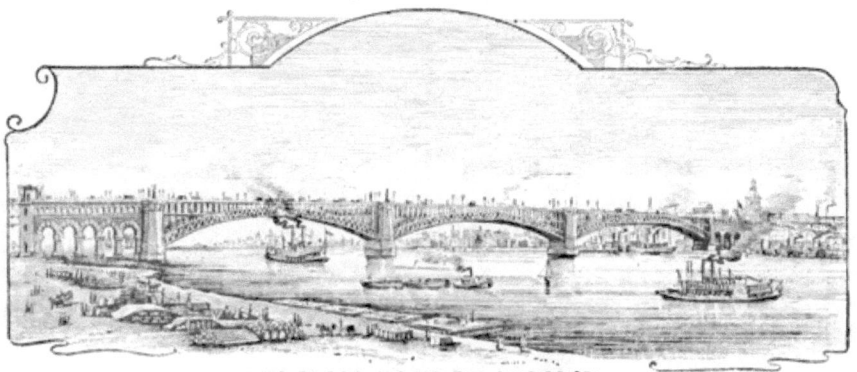

EADS BRIDGE, ACROSS THE MISSISSIPPI.

station in the world. Controlled and operated by a stock company, independent of any specific railroad, it is thereby removed from the individual influence and bias of any one railway corporation. Each railroad entering here is a lessee in common, and thus to each is guaranteed and secured equal rights and just dealings. In architectural skill, genius of workmanship, art in finish, and conception on the part of its promoters, this railway station is a monument imposing, attractive, and highly commendatory.

Delightful for situation, the city of St. Louis ranks as one of the foremost in commerce, manufactures, and in the arts and sciences. Located on the west bank of the renowned Mississippi river, nearly midway between its source and its mouth, no city in the south, west, or southwest can rival it in its importance as an almost unlimited commercial centre. It has 2800 miles of nav-

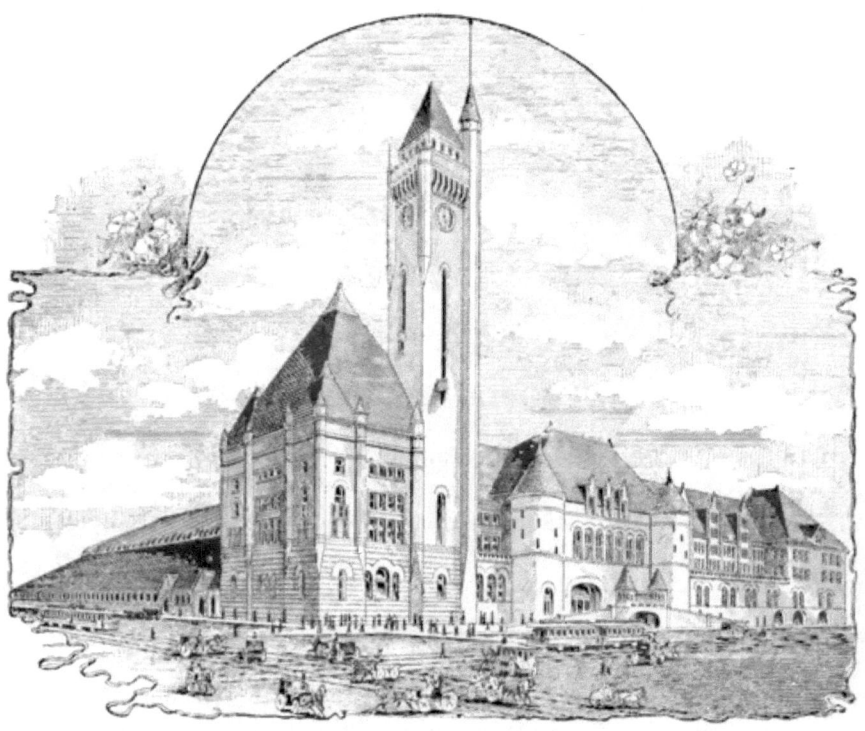

UNION RAILWAY STATION, ST. LOUIS.

igable water-ways, with large and important passenger and freight steamship lines to the city of St. Paul in the middle northwest, and the city of New Orleans in the south. Twenty-one trunk lines of railway terminate here, bringing this city into touch with all the prominent populous centres.

The city, too, is magnificent in its layout, having broad regular and well-paved streets, lined with ornate and imposing residences, and substantial, costly and effective business blocks, churches, and other public buildings. In hotels this city is par-excellence, the commercial man, the tourist, or occasional visitor here finding unsurpassed accommodations. Travellers of wide range and experience speak of the parks and recreation grounds of St. Louis as of the finest in the world, and the beauty, extent, and attractions of these, as also the extreme care devoted to them, receive most flattering mention.

Good-cheer, welcome, hospitality, and a cordial courtesy are emphatically manifest, and the tourist and stranger who visits St. Louis departs with a reluctance, and with an earnest of heart to repeat the visit. It is an enviable position which this celebrated city holds amid her sister cities, and delightful as it is to tarry here, we are admonished that our trip, as planned from home, is still incomplete, and we must pursue our journey. After an excellent supper at the café in the railway station we board our Wagner and depart on the Iron Mountain route, and still further push on into the southwest.

St. Louis to Hot Springs

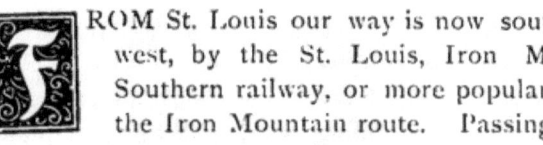ROM St. Louis our way is now south and southwest, by the St. Louis, Iron Mountain and Southern railway, or more popularly known as the Iron Mountain route. Passing out from the city our journey follows, for a long distance, beside the meandering and attractive banks of the Mississippi river. Evening shades obscure our vision, preventing a view of this charming water-way. On our return trip, however, it is our privilege to pass here in the clear, morning light. Our trip, replete with interest, is enhanced as our eyes rest upon this broad, sparkling river. It is a renowned stream, fabled in song and in story, and it engages our attention, and holds and delights us. This, the principal river of North America, has its rise away up in the highlands of the State of Minnesota, 1680 feet above the level of the Gulf of Mexico, into which, after its long flow, it finds its outlet. First brought to notice in the spring of 1541 by Fernando DeSoto, the noted Spanish discoverer, it has since become one of the most famous watercourses of the world. Its Indian or original name, *Miche Sepe*, signifies Great River or Father of Waters. Flowing mostly southerly, with windings to the southwest, it measures from source to mouth, 3160 miles, and is navigable to the falls of St. Anthony, at Minneapolis, Minn., a distance of 2200 miles. It has an average width of 3000

feet, a depth of from seventy-five to one hundred and twenty feet, and has 1500 navigable branches. A visitor approaching this river, or keeping company with it for a greater or shorter distance, cannot fail of admiring its beauty and its majestic proportions.

The name of its hardy discoverer is perpetuated by DeSoto, a town of 5000 inhabitants, a prosperous, active and happy people. The chief industry of the town is the large machine shops of the Iron Mountain route. This little town is surrounded by high hills and reposes prettily in the valley of the Joachim.

The radiant rippling waters of the Mississippi, are kissed by the luminous sunlight, which reflects back, in crystal splendor, the brightness and beauty of the azure dome. On its placid bosom float numerous craft, conveying passengers and freight in either direction. Attention at once centres upon the steam craft, because these are so different from those which navigate our northern bays and rivers. These boats are not propellers, neither are they side-wheelers, but are, in fact, end-wheelers. Of great breadth, and of capacious carrying power, these peculiar boats make a terrible racket as they progress, with this immense wheel at the stern, extending across nearly or quite the full width of the boat, revolving over and over, raising a wake almost equal to a moderate surf on our exposed New England coast.

With the flat and fertile plains of the State of Illinois on the one side of the river, and the equally rich fields of the State of Missouri on the other, the eye is delighted

without tiring, in looking across far stretches on either side as we ride along.

Charming, picturesque, and indescribable, is the variety of mountain and vale, the numerous streams, the diversified country, and the towns and cities along our way. In this section of our country the character of the city or town, either as to the architecture and finish of the buildings, or the manners and customs of the people, are essentially different as compared with our northern makeup. In this southland the streets are more irregular and less finished; the buildings are less pretentious and ornate, many of them, in fact most of them, being small wooden buildings, failing in alignment upon the street, the effect being to give to a definite locality a material lack in stateliness and general character. The people we meet, while courteous, hospitable and true, are unlike our northern Yankees in social or business life.

Passing on beyond DeSoto by this Iron Mountain route we traverse one of the most charming regions for the beauty of its scenery. For hundreds of miles, amid alternating hills and vales, mountains and valleys, exquisite in their panoramic effect, we speed through the lovely Arcadia valley of Missouri, which is bewitchingly fascinating, walled about by the rugged, steep, high, and majestic Ozark mountains. In company with these delectable surroundings we continue on, mile after mile, and still on, into and across the State of Arkansas. Numerous pretty settlements intersperse this lovely mountainous section, many of which evidence progress, while

some appear to shadow a far better past. We pass through Mineral Point and Irondale, each of which is a small town prettily located. As we glide by Irondale we catch a hasty glance of an old furnace, a relic of the past, and suggesting, in its inactivity, an industry of former times.

We make a brief stop at Bismarck, a lively little town of 1000 inhabitants, distant from St. Louis seventy-five miles, which is a shipping point located in a fertile farming section. Beyond Bismarck is the station of Iron Mountain, a small settlement which derives its name from the famous mountain standing at the right of our track. This mountain is, in fact, "an immense hill of iron ore, of superior quality, and of very strange formations."

One of the more noted localities by which we pass is Pilot Knob. This is a commanding eminence, sheltered beneath which is an old down-fallen village, formerly the home of the miners. At the base of this mountain, and scattered over its sides, are the ruins of old iron works, which were once a considerable industry for this village. This business has long since waned, and desolation is the result. At this spot was enacted one of the most bloody and desperate battle scenes of the late Civil War, between Union troops numbering 1120 under Gen. Hugh B. Ewing, and 20,000 Confederates under command of Gen. Sterling Price.

Just beyond Pilot Knob is a beautiful settlement, comprising a small town of 1000 residents, and called Ironton. The layout of this town is artistic and lovely, and

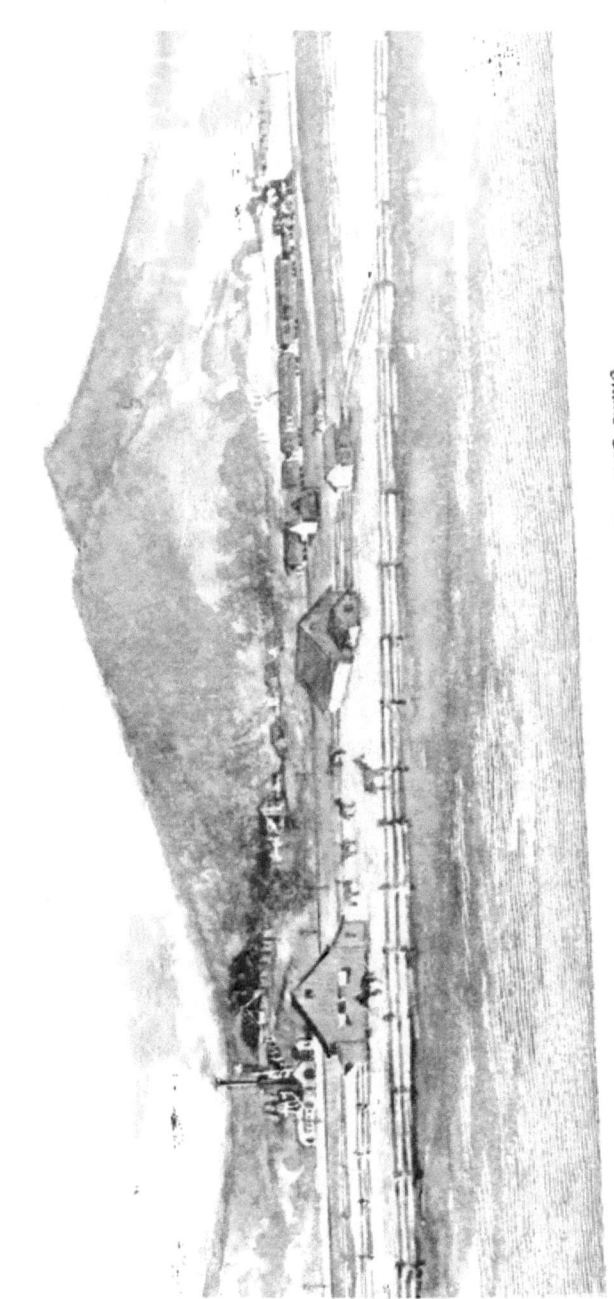

PILOT KNOB AND THE TOWN FROM OLD FORT EWING.

there are many beautiful residences. Of these, that of Judge J. W. Emerson is a "place of great historic interest." The house is large, built of brick, and stands surrounded by spacious grounds beautifully laid out. "The Judge has converted this place into a charming park, with an artificial lake in the centre. There is an old oak tree in the park, shading a fine spring, and it was under this oak that the then Col. Ulysses S. Grant was seated when he received his commission as General in the United States Army. From this point he went to take command at Cairo, and soon after won the victory at Fort Donelson, which was the beginning of his triumphant career. Over the spring is the statue of an angel keeping guard, with an appropiate verse inscribed on the pedestal. The tree is carefully guarded, and a statue near it commemorates the event. The monument is of bronze, on a granite pedestal, and represents a soldier in full uniform resting on his musket. It bears the following inscription :

ERECTED 1886,
BY THE SURVIVING VETERANS OF THE 21ST REGIMENT ILLINOIS VOLUNTEER INFANTRY, TO COMMEMORATE THE SPOT WHERE THEIR COLONEL,

ULYSSES S. GRANT,

RECEIVED HIS COMMISSION AS GENERAL, AND PARTING FROM HIS REGIMENT, ENTERED ON HIS CAREER OF VICTORY,
'LET US HAVE PEACE.'"

The delightful Arcadia valley of Missouri received its name from an eastern lady. After a day's drive, in and

about these charming Ozarks, she was rapturously entertained and impressed with the mountain scenery and its surroundings, and in her delight " she exclaimed ' This is a veritable Arcadia,' and Arcadia it has remained ever since."

Tip-Top on Hogan Mountain, is a noted part of this entrancing spot. This is in the very heart of the Ozarks. On either hand wild vistas of rugged mountain scenery extend, and looking northward the eye is feasted with a magnificent panorama of nature. Below lies the beautiful Arcadia valley, with farmhouses here and there, Shepherd Mountain and Pilot Knob looming up in their conspicuous majesty.

Within about an hour's ride of Tip-Top is Gad's Hill, another captivating site, wildly elegant in its surrounding varied scenery of hill and valley, rocks and shrubbery. Prominence was given to this locality, about twenty-five years ago, as the scene of one of the earliest train robberies by the noted James gang of western desperadoes.

Speeding on, across this interesting section of Missouri, we pass through Piedmont, Mill Spring, Williamsville, Keener's, Poplar Bluff, and Neeleyville. Each of these towns, in their picturesque natural repose, appear as an enchanting resting place to the interested traveller as he leisurely strolls exploring this spell-holding mountainous country.

Poplar Bluff is one of the largest of these settlements, and is a lively and pretty town of 2500 inhabitants. Here we cross the Black river, and follow its right bank

for some forty or fifty miles. The scenery along this river is fine, and the water reflects the sunlight, and beautifully mirrors adjacent objects. The amateur or the expert fisherman may push off from the shore in his boat, and here enjoy excellent sport.

Reaching the border of Missouri, we cross into the State of Arkansas at Moark, distant from St. Louis one hundred and eighty-six miles. This town takes its name from the united abbreviated names of the two States at whose connecting borders it is situated. Jealous and particular are the residents of the State into which we have now entered as to the pronunciation of its name. By official act of the State Legislature, we must say Arkansaw, or we are looked upon with disdain, or regarded as ignoramuses with respect to our linguistic knowledge.

As we have already stated, notable indeed is the change of country, of people, and of every-day life as we now behold it. We who live in New England and the northern section of our country cannot fail of detecting the marked differences between our home life and that as we find it here. Negroes old and Negroes young, Negroes black and Negroes of the mulatto type, make up a large portion, in some instances the greater portion, of the populations of the cities and towns. These people are the direct descendants of the race here in Dixie, who used to sing in their own pathetic dialect and melody :

> " De ole bee make de honey-comb,
> De young bee make de honey,
> De niggers make de cotton en co'n,
> En de w'ite folks gits de money."
> —*Uncle Remus.*

Prolific and fruitful are these sable inhabitants: children numerous, ranging gradually up, like a flight of stairs, hover about the doorsteps of the homes. And these homes —so unlike anything known to us in the north to be called homes—are a marvel viewed from almost any point of consideration. Small, one-story buildings, many of them having but a single room, roughly constructed, unattractive to us in association with the sacred name of "home," as New Englanders prize and understand it,— difficult, indeed, is it for us to comprehend how these people can thus live. What is true in this regard of the colored people of the south is equally as true of the poorer class of the whites. Someone has said that "home is home, be it ever so homely," and these southern homes mentioned are certainly homely and humble.

Drawn to the closest limit is the color line in this southland. At the different railway stations at which we stop we observe that there are two waiting-rooms for passengers, one bearing the word "whites," and the other the word "blacks." About these stations gather large numbers of colored lads, or, as they are sometimes improperly called, "piccaninnies," varying in age from five or six to eighteen or twenty years. They are rudely dressed, are grotesque and slovenly in appearance, but withal bearing a happy and contented countenance. It is our delight to see them tumble all over themselves in their eager anxiety to secure the bright pennies which we throw into their midst. Understanding before we left home that such was "fun alive" for the tourist, we provided

SCRAMBLING FOR PENNIES.

From the Cosmopolitan.

ourselves with a generous supply of these bright pennies, and it is an open question which was the more taken with this sport, we who created it, or those who strove in the scrimmage. Into a dust heap, the dirty roadway, or even into a mud puddle, would these black boys plunge, so eager were they for the possible prize to be secured, and the mix-up of heads and feet, of arms and legs, in this, to us, peculiar diversion, is a sight as comical as it is pleasing.

We make a limited stop at Little Rock, and here partake of a nice breakfast in the café at the railway station, which is called "Pratt's Hotel." This is the capital city of the State, with a population of 40,000, and is a city of prominence in the south, with fine homes, hotels, public buildings and good streets. Of the public buildings, the Old State House is an interesting specimen. Classic and ancient in its architecture, it rivets and holds the attention of the visitor as a worthy relic of by-gone days. Sometimes called the City of Roses, it is a pleasant fact that the residence portion of Little Rock, almost to a house, is beautiful with its flora about the homes, from the early blooms of the spring to the later flowers of the fall, roses and chrysanthemums being prominent in their season. This city is three hundred and forty-five miles from St. Louis, and as we approach it we obtain a good view of it from the car window. Just before reaching this city we cross the Arkansas river, on the south bank of which it is located, and which river is one of the larger and more important affluents of the Mississippi.

LOOKING WEST FROM BIG ROCK, ARK.

Little Rock, as a designation, was first applied to this place by the flatboatmen of early times, who, coming up the river from New Orleans, moored their boats at a projecting rock by the river side, and landing camped out on the banks of the Arkansas. Thus did they name this spot Little Rock, in contra-distinction to another and larger promontory but a short distance further up the river which they designated Big Rock, and these names have ever since held. On the summit of Big Rock, on a level plateau extending a mile or more, the United States Government has established a military post of the first order, with a reservation of 1000 acres of land.

Just as we enter Little Rock we pass the State Penitentiary, prettily located on a hill, the walls of the institution, "with their slowly patrolling armed guards and watchtowers," being observable from the car windows.

A pleasant incident of our trip at this station was the liberal presentation of pretty bouquets of roses and other lovely flowers to the ladies of our party, by the officials of the Iron Mountain route.

From Little Rock we continue on to Malvern, traversing a portion of country of great sameness, attractive, yet sparsely settled, but failing to appeal to us as desirable either for a habitation or for an investment. It is a wooded section, forest and clearing constantly alternating on either side of our swiftly moving train. Sawmills are numerous, with immense heaps of saw-dust all about them, and these mills are busy in the sawing of logs into building timber.

VIEWS ON THE OUACHITA RIVER.

Arrived at Malvern, we are now three hundred and eighty-eight miles from St. Louis. We deflect here from the regular prescribed route of our journey to make a special visit of a day to the world-wide famous city of Hot Springs. Our train is switched from the main road, and we proceed by the Hot Springs railroad, a distance of twenty-two miles, this short cut proving one of the interesting parts of our full-of-interest trip. On this brief length of railway we pass through a picturesque country, and in a level stretch obtain an enchanting view of the glassy and brilliant Ouachita river, with its lovely nooks, its secluded glens, its wooded banks,— the haunt of the lovers, and the retreat of the nature-studying rambler. Crossing Cove Creek, near its sleepy old saw-mill, we make a brief stop at Lawrence station. Off from here, and the stretches of land on either side teem with attractions to our eager, scrutinizing eyes. The Gulpha, a radiant, sparkling rivulet, is a companion with us a large part of the way. This pretty, irregular, winding stream, now flowing over pebbles and rocks, here widening out into small pools or miniature lakes, is beautiful for the reflective clearness of its waters and for its charming natural formation. It is a tributary stream of the Ouachita river, and as it ripples along its way it shimmers and glistens in the sunlight, its reflectant waters mirrowing surrounding hills, shrubbery, and moving objects, the whole blending into a panoramic picture of weird art and natural beauty.

Reaching Hot Springs early in the morning, we have the day before us for prospecting. We are met by a recep-

tion committee representing the Odd Fellows of this city, by whom we are taken in hand, with the evident design from the start that we are to be royally entertained,— a result which we could not dispute when the day was over.

Hot Springs, Arkansas, "The Carlsbad of America," is owned by the United States Government, or, properly speaking, that section embacing within it these "hot springs," and is under the direct supervision of the Department of the Interior. These natural boiling springs, giving to this city its name, are one of the wonders of the world, and this locality has consequently a reputation bounded only by civilization. No more interesting, marvellous and inexplainable phenomenon is to be anywhere found.

Although but a few years, comparatively, since these natural springs, with their miraculous healing properties, have been extensively known and used, yet their discovery extends back to a remote period. Fernando DeSoto, before mentioned as the hardy Spanish explorer, in company with the aboriginees, amid his first explorations, discovered these springs in the early part of the year 1541. As time lapsed, squatters and pioneer settlers began to here construct their rude homes. By virtue of descent from families who early settled on this "Hot Springs Reservation" there were rival claims to ownership of this landed property. These claims, in some instances at least, appear to have been a grab game, right of possession being asserted without apparent just reason. Not

THE HOTEL EASTMAN, HOT SPRINGS.

infrequently such possession was maintained by force of arms, some of the earlier residents holding their property by a sort of shot-gun rule. These questionable holds continued through many years, and finally narrowed down to three prominent claimants. So recent as the year 1877 the United States Court of Claims decided against these claimants. Under this decision, the United States Government, by Act of Congress, appointed a Commission which finally determined these contested rights, and fixed a price to be paid by the settlers upon the " Hot Springs Reservation." At that time there was a resident population here of about 4000. This was the real beginning of the city of Hot Springs, as under this Commission the city was laid out. The streets thus established were made to conform to original lines, as planned and used by early settlers, as also to conform to the peculiar natural topography of the locality.

It is well that the United States Government owns and controls the landed property from which these wonderful springs gush forth. Embraced within this entire Reservation are 2560 acres, the springs, however, being within a limit of 888.7 acres. On April 20, 1832, our National Government, by an Act of Congress, set apart and dedicated to the people of the United States this National Reservation as an American sanitarium.

Hot Springs, as it exists to-day, is a pleasant, active city of 15,000 inhabitants, possessing features distinctive and original unto itself. It is located nearly territorially central of the State of Arkansas, four hundred and ten

MAIN ENTRANCE AND PARK.

INTERIOR OF LOBBY.
EASTMAN BATH HOUSE.

EASTMAN HOTEL VIEWS.

miles southwest of St. Louis, in the heart of the forest-clad Ozark Mountains. It occupies highly elevated ground, being 1000 feet above the sea level, is free from all malarial influences and miasmetic effects, and possesses a climate probably the most equable of any in the United States.

In 1829 the first bath-house was built, and by this definite means these wonderful waters, with their healing powers, were made systematically available to diseased and suffering humanity. The early growth and development of Hot Springs was slow, nevertheless large numbers of invalids every year sought the beneficent helps of this heaven-given panacea. The fame, the extent of use of these springs, and the curative effects here secured, are, however, matters of recent history. In 1874 the Hot Springs railway was built, tapping the Iron Mountain route at Malvern, thus bringing this health-giving natural sanitarium into touch with all the world. Since that time, a little more than twenty years, this thriving city has really come into existence. It possesses all of the features of the average metropolis, with its banks, large and unsurpassed hotels, daily newspapers, numerous churches, public schools, liveries, marts of trade, etc. It has lodges of the foremost secret societies, is prominent in charitable and philanthropic work, and is up-to-date with its electric cars, lights, and varied modern appliances, sewerage, fire, police, and other public departments.

Prospecting about the city, the mountains rising majestically on either hand, we note particularly and admire the pleasing irregularity of the streets, following the natural trend of the hill and the valley. Central avenue, which is the main thoroughfare of the city, was originally the valley running north and south between the Hot Springs Mountain and West Mountain, and was the natural conduit of the Hot Springs Creek. At great expense, in removing boulders and in excavations, the

CENTRAL AVENUE, LOOKING NORTH.

United States Government has placed this creek in a tunnel, in alignment with the avenue which they built above it. This avenue is also the principal business street, and on it are located most of the stores, large blocks, bathhouses, hotels and other public buildings. Many of the blocks are of good size, are of modern style, and are ornamental and substantial in finish, as also there are numer-

PARK HOTEL, HOT SPRINGS.

ous fine residences within the city. Collectively, however, the buildings are incongruous, irregular in alignment, and symmetry and grace are not apparent in the "make-up." Fine brick blocks alternate with low, dingy, one-story shanties, and beauty in business blocks and in homes and adjacent grounds is marred by uncompanionable, dilapidated wooden buildings, and neglected and run-down so-called homes. The rural and the elegant thus go hand-in-hand. Time, however, cannot fail to

OLD HALE SPRING.

correct, and indeed is rapidly correcting, this incongruity and negligence. We are, nevertheless, pleased with the city, and find the residents to be affable, kind, hospitable, and alert with courtesy and genuine welcome at every turn.

The celebrated hot springs come from the mountain at numerous places, the rock all about the outlets exhibiting formations, due to the flow of the water, which are exquisite in crystalline and brilliantly reflective gems. Stalac-

IN FRONT OF THE ARLINGTON.

GRAND STAIRWAY, HOT SPRINGS MOUNTAIN.

PROMENADE, GOVERNMENT RESERVATION.

tites, carbonates, and diamonds from Hot Springs are quite extensively used in the jewelry trade, the claim being made that an expert can scarcely detect the difference between the "real" and the Hot Springs diamond. The immensity of flow of the water from these springs seems almost incredible, amounting to 840,000 gallons daily, and varying in temperature, as separately located, from

ENTRANCE TO CLOSED SPRING, ON THE
HOT SPRINGS MOUNTAIN.

ninety-six to one hundred and fifty-seven degrees farenheit. These waters proceed from the Hot Springs Mountain, an end or attachment of the Ozark Mountains, and as they issue, they unceasingly gurgle, bubble and boil, mysteriously coming from a source hidden and unknown, and heated by a cause known only to the Supreme Creator.

Tanks in the mountain side have been constructed, as reservoirs of deposit, into which these waters are conducted and stored. Bath houses have been built in direct connection with the springs, and money has been expended without stint to bring these waters into service for the benefit and health of humanity. Hotels have been constructed, which are palatial, elegant, and costly, lacking

BATH HOUSE ROW ON GOVERNMENT RESERVATION.

in nothing conducive to comfort, convenience, and luxury, and connected with each of which and forming a part of the structure is a bath-house. No finer hostelries can be found the wide world over, and certainly none which contemplate in their construction so much for guests in physical enjoyment and improvement.

With one exception, all of the hot springs flow from the

Hot Springs Mountain, on the east side of Central avenue. A common reservoir has been constructed to which these naturally flowing waters are conducted by underground pipe lines, thus economizing the supply for distribution to the several bath-houses. Bath-house row is a popular section of the east side of Central avenue. It comprises a continuous row of ten bath-houses, all located on the Hot Springs Mountain Reservation. Exteriorly this row is a charm in combination, and in architecture is unique and pretty. The buildings are set back from the avenue, and in front of them is an exquisite little park about a quarter of a mile long and one hundred feet wide. These bath-houses are unexcelled by any other structure called a bath-house to be found in the United States. Contiguous to, connected with, and in some instances attached to the hotels, these bath-houses range in cost from $10,000 to $50,000 each.

BATHER.

One of the most prominent in design, in beauty, in size, and in completeness, is the United States Government Free Bathhouse. This is, as its name implies, free to suffering American subjects unable, on account of lack of financial means, to pay the expense attendant upon the privilege of these healing baths, who are thus permitted, under certain regulations, to have the gracious benefits of these curative waters at public expense. It is a most worthy public charity.

There are a number of other of these celebrated bath-houses within the city which are not located directly on the Government Reservation. Conception in appointments appears to have been supreme. Apparently nothing is lacking to render these famous resorts all that can be desired for invalids,— to bathe, to drink, or in any wholesome way, as directed by the physician, to use these health-giving waters. Not alone, however, are these renowned baths sought exclusively by the diseased and the afflicted, but hundreds of people here visit to plunge into these natural hot waters for the comfort, delight, stimulation and vigor which they impart to the system.

Constructed of brick, stone, and other fine materials, with interior finish in marble and choice hard woods, these bath-houses, as also the large hotels, which are in part bath-houses, are buildings of splendor and artistic mechanism. Each of them are divided interiorly into a number of apartments, and are provided with large pool baths, ordinary bath-tubs, vapor baths, douché baths, hot room, drying-rooms provided with willow couches and chairs, and all accessories necessary to the completion of every feature appertaining to a professional bath. Under the direction of expert physicians, of wide and skillful experience, a most careful and rigid diagnosis is made of every case, and ills which are invulnerable to other modes of medical treatment yield to the magic touch of these life-giving hot springs. So-called incurables go forth from here with a new lease of life, and with years of health and comfort supplementing, it may be, years of disease and misery. These bath-houses have a number of attaches, mostly colored servants, who conduct the patients through the various forms of the bath, furnishing attentive personal care, a no small feature of which is a vigorous rubbing down with a rough bath towel which sends the life current tingling and flowing through the veins.

About the city, at frequent intervals, are handsome fountains, artistic in design, which are furnished with a number of drinking cups. Steadily flowing from these fountains, through numerous openings, is the clear, crystal water. This is not only warm water, but is, in fact, hot, and the residents approaching fill a cup and drink with as much apparent relish and satisfaction as we northern people quench our thirst with ice water.

AN ATTENDANT.

The Government maintains an extensive, imposing,

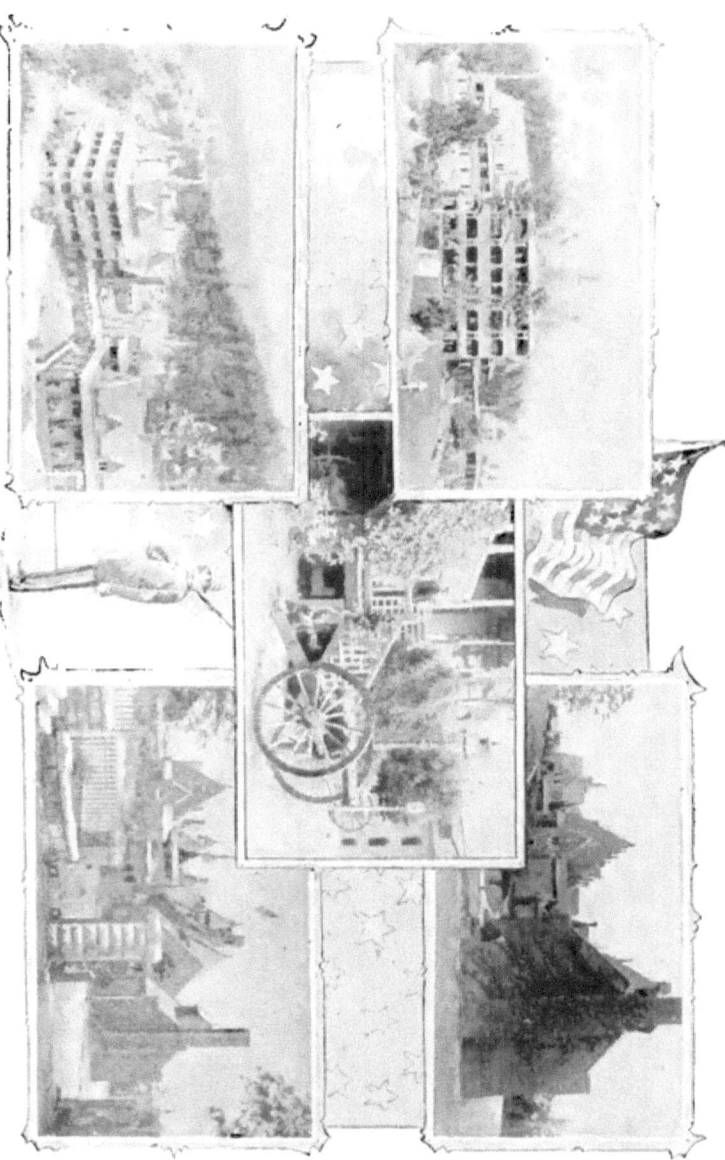

THE UNITED STATES ARMY AND NAVY HOSPITAL, HOT SPRINGS.

GRAND ENTRANCE TO UNITED STATES ARMY AND NAVY HOSPITAL.

and magnificent Army and Navy Hospital at Hot Springs. Its equal is not to be found in the world. Located well up on the mountain slope, it is a structure not only attractive but elegant, and the tourist may linger about it and gaze rapturously upon it, or he may enter it and examine it in its completeness, the while he is courteously told its object and the work which it is doing, and from any point of observation which he may view or consider it, he cannot fail of admiration and inspiration, and feel swelling within him gratitude to the glorious American nation which founded and sustains it. An abundance of naturally beautiful grounds all about this Hospital are lavishly and tastefully adorned with shrubbery and flowering plants, natives and exotics, which at once transform these grounds into a lovely spot, a delight not only to the eye, but an artistic study for the mind. The drives and walks about the Hospital and grounds are a chain of enchantment, and a source of never-failing delight.

Residing on the Government Hot Springs Reservation is a Superintendent, appointed by the Secretary of the Interior, who has charge of all the Government interests here, and he is constant in his care, and energetically faithful in regulating and improving this property. Money has been, and is constantly, lavishly spent in developing and beautifying all of this public reservation.

As before noted, the Hot Springs hotels are of the best. The larger ones are The Eastman, The Arlington, and The Park. These elaborate hostelries without their attached bath-house could not long exist. During our brief tarry

THE ARLINGTON HOTEL, HOT SPRINGS.

INTERIOR VIEWS ARLINGTON HOTEL, HOT SPRINGS.
INTERIOR OF THE LOBBY. GRAND STAIRWAY. THE ORCHESTRA. THE MAIN VERANDA.

MAIN DINING HALL, THE ARLINGTON.

for the day our headquarters are at The Arlington, and we cannot forego the pleasure of a brief descriptive word. This hotel is the only one located on the Government Reservation, and occupies the northwest corner. It is new, and was opened to the public March 25, 1893. It cost $550,000, and displaced the old Arlington, a very much smaller and unpretentious structure. This new hotel fronts six hundred and fifty feet on Central avenue and Fountain avenue, it is four stories high, and is constructed of brick, stone and iron. From each of the two principal corners rises a tower twenty feet square, extending forty feet above the roof, from the interior of which observations of unsurpassed loveliness of nature may be had. At the rear of the hotel the verdure clad Hot Springs Mountain rises majestically to an altitude of upwards of five hundred feet. A description of the accessories and appointments of this hotel is unnecessary here; it is quite enough to say that everything for the comfort, convenience, and pleasure of the guest, has been provided. The bath-house attached is simply elegance itself, and complete for its purposes to the amplest degree. The interior finish of the building, the size, height, accommodations and furnishings of the rotunda, the parlors, the dining-rooms, the guest chambers, in fact every feature and part of the building is all that modern skill and art can devise and provide. Its manager, Mr. Lyman T. Hay, is a host affable, genial, and attentive, — in the fullest meaning of these terms — to the guest and to the invalid. He is comparatively a young man, and, under his management, this hotel is a pronounced success.

LADIES ASSEMBLY ROOM. THE ARLINGTON.

LADIES PINK PARLOR, THE ARLINGTON.

Our tarry and our entertainment here will never fade from memory, and the Menu which we enjoyed in the elegant dining-room at noon and at evening, in a wide experience, was never more palatable or better served.

The social life at Hot Springs is cultured, refined, and enjoyable. Visitors meet here from all over our country and from foreign lands; amusements are never lacking; entertainment and receptions are frequent, and thus the social touch, development and acquaintance of this mountain city is constantly of the broadest influence and most helpful character.

A ride about the city, and a drive up the winding side of the Hot Springs Mountain, afforded a joyful experience which will be a meditative pleasure throughout life.

To speak of a visit to Hot Springs and not mention Happy Hollow, would be like the play of "Hamlet with Hamlet left out." This is a charmed spot, the haunt of the ruralist, and the retreat of the naturalist. It is not a dale nor a glen, neither is it a natural ravine or valley, but is rather a "flat roadway hewn from the side of the mountain." Here the tourist may revel amid nature's beauties, and fancy himself, in retrospective imagination, in the midst of and surrounded by the mythical gods and goddesses, the nymphs and dryads of Grecian antiquity. It is, indeed, a fit resort for ye naiads and ye queens, ye fairies and ye Lilliputians, of both ancient and modern times. A famous retreat for the pedestrian, it is also one of the delightful drives of this wonderful locality.

DRIVES ON THE HOT SPRINGS MOUNTAIN.

Happy Hollow Springs, at the end of the driveway, is an enchanting issue of water from the mountain, not hot, like most of its neighboring springs, but a mineral water of high degree, possessing healthful and curative properties. Beyond here, up the mountain side, it is steep, rugged, jagged, difficult of ascent, but possessing a weird fascination to the hardy and interested roamer among nature's wonders.

DRIPPING SPRINGS.

In and about Hot Springs, in its suburban districts, are many other lovable and attractive haunts. Detailed narration of these within the scope of this sketch is denied. Partially enumerated they are Potash-sulphur Springs, Mountain Valley Springs, Lake Hotel and Springs, Henry's Bonanza Springs, Gillen's White Sulphur Springs, Hell's Half Acre, and the Thousand Dripping Springs,— each of which are possessed of natural beauty and sublime attractions sufficient to hold the spell-bound tourist in admiration and voluntary gratitude to the Divine Creator.

Overhanging a roadway and issuing from almost innumerable crevices in the rocky ledge, the Thousand Dripping Springs gush and trickle, each, apparently, representing a separate spring.

HELL'S HALF ACRE.

Hell's Half Acre is marvellously grand in its fated loneliness, and is a spot majestic in its original grandeur. Comprising an acre or thereabouts, it is not a chasm but a depression, a yawning abyss, sinking to a depth of from ten to thirty feet below the earth's surface. Huge boulders, jagged rocks—multitudinous in shape, color, and kind—brush and shrubbery, combine in presenting a site captivating alike for the naturalist and visitor, which is indescribably wild and bewitching.

Opportunities for horse-back riding and for carriage drives are of the most fascinating sort at Hot Springs. The variety of the turn-outs and the equestrian equipages are pleasingly attractive for their dissimilarity,—their elegance and their rudeness. The donkey rider or driver is

DONKEY DRIVERS AT THE SPRINGS.

apparently as much " in it," for the real joy of the ride, as is he who, nattily and prettily attired, sits astride the graceful saddle-horse, or he who, in his broadcloth and silk hat, draws the reins over the finest liveried tandem or span.

This is truly one of the many entrancing haunts for the tourist in our broad and loved America, and is interestingly romantic for all that it affords of natural beauty and man's artistic genius, both in the city of Hot Springs and in its environs.

But evening has come, we say good-bye at the railway station to our committee of friends who have made the day so pleasant and instructive to us; the conductor shouts "all aboard," we are off, and soon are back to Malvern, where, striking the main road, we continue by the Iron Mountain route still further towards the southwest.

OF WHICH MANY ARE SEEN IN DIXIE.

Hot Springs to Dallas

VENING is well advanced as we leave Malvern, with Dallas, the objective city towards which we are journeying, but about twelve hours' ride ahead of us. Each revolution of our car wheels, as we glide along, seems in concert to say,—"far-away, far-away, far-away,"— and in the imaginative echo we fully realize the fact that home and our every-day personal interests are many miles back of us.

Continuing on from Malvern, darkness denies us a view of the landscape, which, however, we obtain on our way back, several days later, as we then pass here by daylight. We find that we ride through a wooded country, and indications point to a once large growth of timber, which must have been a prominent industrial factor here, but the tireless axeman has felled most of the trees, and, as a result, rough, stumpy land is all about us. Something of this industry still remains, and saw-mills in operation are quite frequent, but these, as apparently conducted, do not manifest an over-thriving business. Dull and quiet indeed does the whole neighborhood appear, and but little inspiration is imparted. To add to the evident quietude of the entire surroundings, lazy old mules mope listlessly about in the unfertile pastures, or stand at intervals, sleepily indolent, unmoved by our passing train, and apparently oblivious to all adjacent objects, and stupidly indifferent to all environments. There is, nevertheless, a happy exception to this almost universal dearth and inactivity. Here and there, lots cleared of stumps and stones, show a luxuriant growth of fruits, berries, vegetables, and other agricultural products, which betokens a thrift and a frugality which is at once appreciated and commended.

These large States in the southwest, through which we journey, with the many miles of unoccupied land, with the occasional small settlements through which we pass, make a decided effect upon us in contrast with the thickly settled and busy portions of our familiar north. Low, one-story buildings are, in the towns here, the rule rather than the exception, and these buildings, with an occasional taller and more impressive neighbor, are unpretentious and irregular. The so-called streets appear to us more like ungraded highways, and there is a lack of harmony in design, finish, and alignment. Yet in this incongruity there is a charm, the variety of architecture is an attraction, and the apparent neglect of survey and contour is of itself an interesting feature.

Here the climate is warm, the houses are without basements, and are set on brick pillars or wooden posts— mostly the latter — the doors of the homes are open, presenting to us a "homely home" interior, and the residents about the doorsteps and around the premises, in dress and in manners, are to us of far different domestic appearance than we are accustomed to. In these humble, small, low homes, whites and blacks live together, as

From the Cosmopolitan.

A TYPICAL SOUTHERN NEGRO HOME

neighbors, in evident acclimation, and appear to be a contented people.

Our large department stores, mammoth groceries, tall and stately blocks filled with the various lines of business offices, in the large towns and cities with which we are familiar, impress us, as never before, with their magnificence and their industrial significance, as we now, in these towns in our southwest, observe so many rude, rough, one-story, one-room, wooden buildings, with a sign over the entrance reading, respectively, " Dry Goods," " Groceries," and the like. The contrast is painfully striking.

It is to be remembered, however, that in a most important sense, this is a new section of country, and that a new life is opening up to this people under conditions diametrically opposite to such as have been previously dominant here. While the differences noted in the people and in the make-up of these settlements are true, it is yet nevertheless undeniably true, that there are here in this southwest many buildings of modern design, with evidences of business push and success, as also pretty and well improved homes, the whole signifying a progressive citizenship, and auguring for the future a solid and permanent growth. We are impressed and delighted, as we alight for a few moments as the train stops at different stations, to meet and talk with the residents, and we detect in them a hospitable, kind, and courteous people.

Another, to us, strange sight, novel and attractive, greets our ever insatiate vision. Almost all the way,

ARKADELPHIA, ARK., FROM NORTH BANK OF OUACHITA RIVER.

through the country districts, since leaving Malvern, we behold in the open lots, in the highways, by the homes, and even along the line of the railway by which we travel, large numbers of black, razor-back hogs, roaming and feeding, indifferent to all about them, and apparently altogether "at home" wherever they choose to meander. This, of course, as it seems to us, is a direct breach of domestic existence, and such as at home would be prohibited by law.

The radiant, sparkling, reflective Ouachita river, before mentioned, is again a companion with us, and we cross it at Arkadelphia, where we make a brief tarry at the railway station. We obtain a good view of this town, and are most favorably impressed with it. To all appearances it is a flourishing settlement, evidencing a prosperous and peaceful community.

Continuing on, we enter a pine grove, and we pass through Gurdon, Prescott and Hope, each of which are delightful for situation amid the surrounding forest. We admire the tall, straight, majestic trees for their beauty, and they indicate a comfortable retreat. The density of this forest is pleasantly relieved by occasional clearings, dotted with fields under cultivation, rich in fruitage, and showing care and skill in tillage. The lumbering interests are prominent in this section, and large mills and lumber yards are in evidence on either side of our train.

To add to the charm of the diversified landscape, numerous fertile cotton fields engage and hold our atten-

AWAY DOWN IN DIXIE.

IN THE COTTON FIELD

tion. These are a novelty peculiarly fascinating to our eyes, unaccustomed, as they are, to such scenes. The cotton plants, covering the fields, are in different stages of maturity, and are graceful in their variety of bud, blossom and fruit. The bud is, in appearance, a hard, green ball, while the bloom is lovely in its color of magenta or light purple, with its delicate streaks of lighter and darker shades. At maturity we find in place of the blossom, a bunch of pure, soft cotton, enclosing the cotton seed. As we look at this soft, downy ball, we instinctively turn, for a comparison, to the cotton garments which we wear, and, as mystical as it appears, we nevertheless fully realize that these same cotton garments are undeniably a vegetable product. Not here, but before we return home, we are permitted to obtain, from the cotton field, samples of this wonderful plant in its different stages of growth. Working hither and yon, in these pretty fields of varying color, "the cotton-picking darkies" labor, and furnish by their presence, mingled with the natural beauty of the scene, a real picture in color which is very gratifying. These persistent, tireless toilers, gather the cotton into baskets depositing it at a convenient spot on the field in one general heap, which, at a distance, appears much like a snowbank, — the latter, however, being something quite unknown in this locality.

Four hundred and seventy-one miles from St. Louis we arrive at Fulton, a small, typical southern town. Here we cross the Red river, one of the prominent watercourses of the southwest, and the lowest western branch

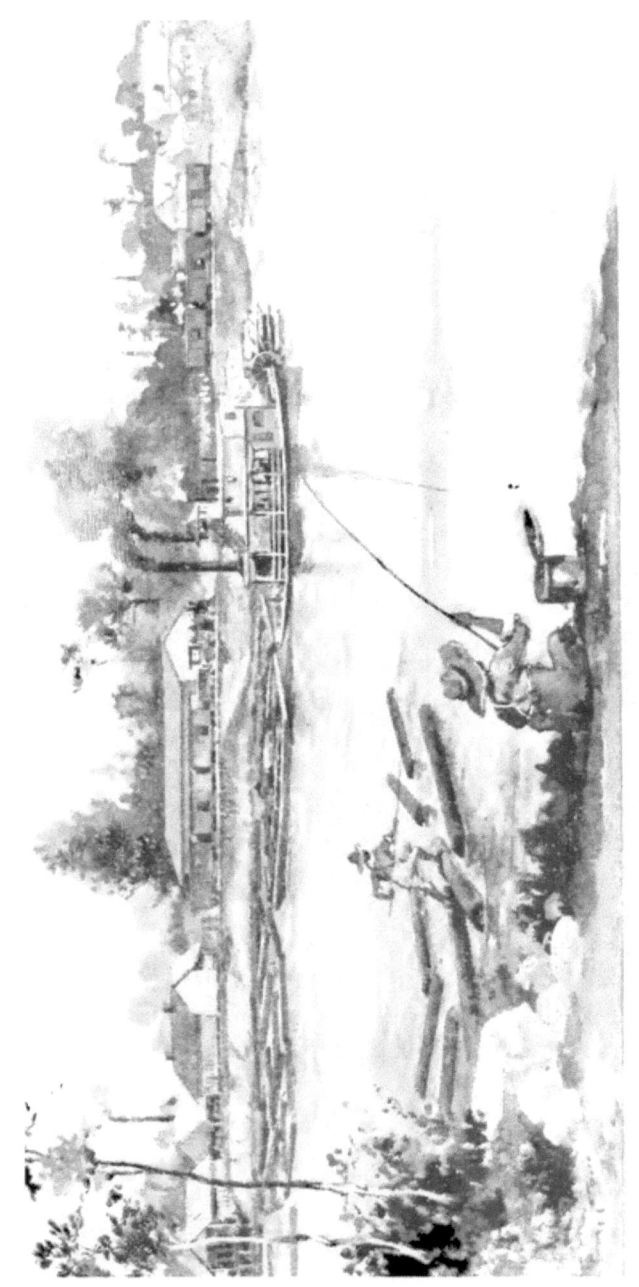

of the matchless Mississippi. This river is 2100 miles long, and loses itself in the Mississippi three hundred and forty-one miles above the mouth of the "father of waters." It makes the boundary line between New Mexico and Texas, and for sixty miles above its mouth it is especially picturesque in its flow between perpendicular banks ranging from six hundred to eight hundred feet in height. Season has much to do with navigation upon this river, and for eight months of the year it is navigable as far as Shreveport, Louisiana. As we cross it, and glance down upon its waters, we readily discover the significance of its name, derived, as it is, from the reddish soil over and through which it flows, and with which its waters are impregnated. Old, dilapidated, and forsaken little steamboats, shadowing in their worn-out appearance indications of better days, can occasionally be seen at Fulton, moored along side the bank, the only craft, being built for the service, that could ascend this river to this point. Railroads have despoiled these "navigators" of their occupation, and the few that remain exist simply as relics of what they have been and what they were to commerce here. By their agency, Fulton once enjoyed a considerable commercial importance, and by them the large cotton crop of the "Red river bottoms" was freighted for distribution to different markets.

Leaving Fulton we proceed for nineteen miles and then stop before the imposing railway station at Texakarna. We are now four hundred and ninety miles from St. Louis, and are at the border of the two great States of

Arkansas and Texas. In fact, as our train halts, about half of it is in each of the two States. This, the so-called gateway to the further west and southwest, is one of the most important railway centres of the extensive southwest. Its name, as is at once suggested, is derived from the two States which it separates; or, singularly as it may appear, and more properly speaking, the two States which it unites; for it is in fact a united territory, and

RAILWAY STATION, TEXAKARNA. IRON MOUNTAIN ROUTE.

in reality two cities, each bearing the same name, and respectively located in the States of Arkansas and Texas. Each city has its separate municipal government, and the mayor of either city, thus peculiarly situated in allied yet disunited communities, is supreme in his vested authority within his individual settlement, and may yet come together for conviviality and social fellowship under conditions and circumstances dissimilar to any other American populated centre. The railway station at Texakarna is of brick, symmetrical in its architecture, is ample and convenient, and it is one of the most ornate and attractive in the southwest. Midway of its length is a wide, high archway, for passage of pedestrians and carriages, which marks the border line between the two States which hold this station in joint possession. Taking a dinner here in the café, we found the table service to be excellent, and its cuisine of the best.

Entering Texas, and proceeding southwest and then nearly west, for a distance of two hundred and twenty-two miles, we reach Dallas, "the pride of the Lone Star State," the city towards which we have travelled nearly 2000 miles since leaving home. From Texakarna to Dallas we pass through, as principal towns, Jefferson, Marshall, Longview, and Mineola, each of which are characteristically typical of this section. The topography of the country passed is similar to that of other parts of this southland, of which we have previously spoken. Notwithstanding the long distance covered, the many objects of constant absorbing interest observed *en-route*, these terminating miles of our trip are filled with never ceasing dissolving views which are delightfully entertaining.

Texas is a magnificent State from many points of consideration. It has a proud heritage, and has an honorable history in which the native Texan exultingly glories. It is separated from the Republic of Mexico by the majestic Rio Grande, which flows between and washes the shores of these two vast divisions of country. One of the southwestern border States, Texas enjoys the proud distinction of being the largest in the Federal Union. For more than a century and a half it was owned by Spain, and was governed by the Spaniards. After a determined and bloody conflict, struggling for independence from Spanish rule, it became an imperial independent Republic in the spring of 1836, and floated its own separate flag enclosing its individual "lone star." It continued as a distinct Republic until admitted as one of the federated States of the Union in 1845. Espousing the cause of the Southern Confederacy, Texas seceded from the Union February 1, 1861, and was readmitted in 1872.

This immense State measures 265,780 square miles, embracing 175,587,840 acres. Figures are easily written and in speech roll from the tongue without much effort, but reflection upon the vastness of the area of the State of Texas is singularly surprising and impressive. Some conception of the great extent of territory of this State may be had when we consider that if the States of Maine, New Hampshire, Vermont, Massachusetts, Rhode Island, Connecticut, New York, Pennsylvania, New Jersey, Delaware, Maryland, Ohio and Indiana were united into one block they would fall short by several hundred square miles of making the total area of Texas. Texas would make two hundred and twelve States the size of Rhode Island, and yet leave land enough to make more than one-half of another one. Russia, of the European powers, alone exceeds it in size; and it is larger, were they all united, than the kingdoms of England, Ireland, Scotland, Wales, Holland, Belgium, Denmark, Switzerland, Greece, and Turkey.

The State of Texas has a population representing in nativity nearly every State in the Union, with a good proportion of emigrants from most every foreign land. Its soil for the most part is of a thick, black, greasy consistency, and is very rich and fruitful. For many vegetarian purposes it requires no other fertilizer than its own abundant fecundity. The State is also prolific in ores, minerals, limes, etc., these natural deposits being of the best anywhere found. Its growth of cotton, tobacco, sugarcane, berries, fruits, and other vegetable products gives it a valuable and a leading commercial position.

Numerous manufacturing establishments, founderies, and other branches of trade, including cotton mills, grain elevators, meat-packing houses, stores and offices, place this State foremost in industrial pursuits. Fish are plentiful in its many lakes, rivers, and water-courses, and various kinds of game are found in almost every county of the State. It has excellent water supplies all over the State, has a number of artesian wells of great capacity, which yield a water as clear as crystal, and which is prized for its purity for domestic purposes.

Excellent provision has been made for the education of its citizens, the State possessing a large available school fund of upwards of $70,000,000, as an endowment for this purpose.

In a variety of ways, this sovereign State, amid the galaxy of States, is prominent with an honorable prestige which presages, due to its natural resources and the genius of its citizens, a proud rank in the future among the civilized peoples of the world.

The city of Dallas, where we sojourn for a week, is the county seat of Dallas county. Located in the northern part of this prodigous State, this county is one of the third tier of counties south of the Red river. As a county

RESIDENCE OF G. M. DILLEY, DALLAS.

it stands first in taxable values, and thus is the wealthiest and is the most populous of either of the counties in the State. Its altitude is about five hundred feet above sea level. Both the city and county were named in honor of the late Hon. George M. Dallas, of Pennsylvania, Vice-President of the United States during the administration of James K. Polk, from 1845-1849. This honor was bestowed for the interest of Vice President Dallas in the admission of Texas to the Federal Union, and the influence which such proposed admission had upon the election of Polk and Dallas.

We are here in the city of Dallas in attendance upon the seventy-second annual communication of the Sovereign Grand Lodge of Odd Fellows. In consequence of this gathering, hundreds of strangers, as guests, are domiciled here for a week, and we are all graciously received by the citizens. The city is in holiday attire, as this assembly is to them an occasion of much importance, and is cherished by the residents as a distinguished honor.

Our headquarters are at the Oriental Hotel, a large, new structure, in the Renaissance style of architecture, and which cost $600,000. It is under the management of Mr. A. Soule, of New England birth, who proves himself a host indeed, and demonstrates, by an excellent table service, courtesies to guests, and personal attention to individual comforts of his sojourners, that he knows how to keep a hotel. Few hotels, in many of the larger cities of the Union, can equal "The Oriental" in its conveniences, and its capacity. It is the finest hostelry in the southwest, it is built of brick, is six stories high, covering an entire block, is magnificent in its furnishings, and is heated by steam and lighted by electricity. It is centrally located, and is thus convenient to all desirable parts of the city.

Dallas is very much unlike our northern and western cities, lacking in the finish of its streets, uniformity in the character and beauty of its private and public buildings, and in the extent and conduct of its trade. Nevertheless

ORIENTAL HOTEL, DALLAS.

it is an active, pretty southern city, is populous and growing, and has a future full of promise. Like other parts of the south, due to the warm climate, most of its buildings, and especially its homes, are without basements, and are set on low, brick pillars, or wooden posts, allowing a free current of air to pass between the ground and lower floor. The city has a large Negro population, and these and the poorer classes of the whites, as before noted of other sections of this southland, occupy humble homes in low, small, inferior buildings, many of which are reduced to a single room. These homes appear humble and plain indeed, to eyes accustomed to see the poorer people of the north occupying far superior dwellings.

This city is situated on Trinity river, which is formed by the united waters of the West Fork of the Trinity river, the Elm river and Mountain creek, which flow in from the westward. Trinity river, at the site where Dallas is located, is crossed by the Texas and Pacific railway. This city is six hundred and sixty miles from St. Louis, and is three hundred and fifteen from Galveston in the south of Texas on the Gulf of Mexico. The spot occupied by Dallas is especially advantageous for a city, being situated on a level plateau, elevated from twenty to thirty feet above the Trinity river, on the right bank of which it is built. It is, in many ways, a new city. The first settlement here was affected so recently as 1840, and in 1870, when the State of Texas was readmitted to the Union, from which it had seceded on account of the Civil war, there was a resident population in Dallas of only

1700. In 1880 this population had increased to 10,368; in 1890 to 38,067. and is now about 50,000, exhibiting a rapid growth, and which has been healthy, both from a social and business standpoint. The census figures of 1890 gave to this city the position of first rank in the State. It is still rapidly growing, and because of its especially favorable location, it is a sharp rival with sister southern cities for future supremacy, with the odds decidedly in its favor. While many very small and inferior buildings are to be found here, yet it is pleasant to note that these are, from time to time, giving way to more modern and stately blocks, and there is a constant improvement in the style of the homes, and a number of fine residences adorn some of the streets.

Liberal allowance in the layout of this city has been made, its streets and avenues being from eighty to a hundred and twenty feet wide, and these run mostly at right angles. Its industrial interests involve large investments of capital, and these, already numerous, are constantly increasing, and by them employment is furnished to large numbers of both sexes. These industries represent a variety of occupations, averaging well with the diversified pursuits of many older cities of wider opportunities. There are numerous prolific cotton fields within the limits of the city, and this native product is here being passed through the various stages of preparation in order to place it on the market ready for sale from the store counter.

A new and important industry in this city, established within the past year or two, is the slaughtering of beeves and hogs, the stockyards embracing a considerable extent of land. This occupation is growing, and an important feature of it is the packing and hermetical sealing of meats for foreign and domestic trade.

Trinity river, on which the city of Dallas is located, is a narrow stream, and is navigated by small steamboats of peculiar mechanism. It is navigable south for a distance of twenty-two miles towards the gulf of Mexico, Dallas being now at the head of its navigation. The possibilities of this water-course above Dallas to future commercial interests are most promising, and much has been done, at private expense, to increase its navigable resources. Above here, along the banks of this river, and extending back and over a wide territory, are large forests of excellent trees, and with this river widened and dredged so as to float this timber to Dallas, from whence it could be forwarded to various centres of trade, sawmills and planing mills might be erected and operated to a good profit, thus adding to this locality and to this city an important lumber business.

The public departments of the city are well organized, and, in their equipment, are of the latest kind. Prominent of these is the fire department, which is the pride of the State, and it has the Gamewell system of fire alarm, thus giving to the city prompt and reliable notification of a fire. This department is supplemented with a large and well equipped Municipal Water plant, with a daily pumping capacity of 27,000,000 gallons. This city also has an excellent sewerage system with over thirty miles of

VIEWS ON TRINITY RIVER.

laid sewers. In addition to the public water supply there are several private supplies, including a number of artesian wells, extending to a depth of from 700 to 800 feet, and from these several sources the residents have an ample supply of pure, soft, clear water.

A variety of organizations, including the leading secret orders, an influential commercial club, and other organi-

EPISCOPAL COLLEGE, DALLAS.

zations for social, literary, and philanthropic ends, gives to the city an interchange of association and a development of society of high beneficial influence.

In educational matters the city is wide-awake and progressive, the public school system is broad and liberally supported, and there are a number of private academies and colleges for higher education. The different religious denominations are active in Christian and charitable work, with fine church edifices conveniently located, and the professions are prominently in evidence by gymnastic associations, art and musical clubs, etc.

For a city of so recent date, Dallas has a number of fine business blocks and public buildings which would do credit and be an ornament to any municipality. Of these the Court House is the most prominent, and in architecture, in appointments, in completeness and conveniences, is an undisputed model. It was erected at a cost of $350,000. Among other of the more noted of the public buildings are a Club House, costing $88,000; an Opera House, $125,000; and a Mechanics Exchange and City Hall, $83,000. Shade trees, in the residential parts of the city, add beauty to the appearance of the streets, and give comfort to pedestrians. Although situated so far south, Dallas has a comfortable and equable climate, and is regarded above the average as a healthy city.

It is also the greatest jobbing centre of the whole southwest, and is the most important railway centre in this section. Five trunk lines of railway enter this city, radiating to all important points, and emphasize the commercial position of the city. The commercial interests of the city are further subserved by an excellent and complete banking system, a number of banks, of national reputation and large business, being active in the mercantile affairs of Dallas.

In literature Dallas is foremost, the character and number of its newspapers and periodicals being in the lead

COUNTY COURT HOUSE AT DALLAS

as compared with any other part of the vast State in which it is situated. The daily papers published here are bright, newsy, and well-edited, and are metropolitan journals of merit.

Situated here are the headquarters of the Texas State Fair and Dallas Exposition. This is a large and prosperous association, centraly located, with an extensive property, embracing one hundred and twenty-two

GRAND STAND AT FAIR GROUNDS, DALLAS.

acres of land, supplied with the needed buildings, all of modern design, and the entire equipment is maintained in prime condition. Conspicuous of the buildings are a large horticultural hall, an ample machinery hall, a commodious general main building, and stalls sufficient to accommodate thousands of head of live stock. Within these premises are five miles of graveled drives, fine smooth, level walks, and an unsurpassed race course. This property cost over a half million of dollars, and the annual exhibitions of the society are of a high order, are eminently successful, and are attended by from 200,000 to 400,000 persons, not a few of whom come a distance of many miles.

From this outline some conception may be had of the rank and prospective future of this aggressive southwestern city, which now, in the southwest, stands unrivalled in social, commercial and educational lines.

Our leisure time of our limited pilgrimage in Dallas is fully improved in adventure and sight-seeing. New scenes and experiences, pleasurable and instructive, are constantly coming to our view. The city has an equipment of street cars, circling the city and extending into the suburbs, traversing a distance of about twenty-eight miles. By these we cover considerable territory, aiding us materially in prospecting. These cars are indeed unique, novel in their operation, and are not maintained up to the highest standard of appearance. They are all of the "bob-tail" style, each passenger serving as his own conductor, paying fare through a slot into a small box at the front of the car, also reversing the seats for riding in the direction in which the car is going, or serving one's self to any other needed courtesy in connection with the ride.

All of these cars are not electric, far from it; for there are several lines of horse cars. Horse cars, did we say? we must be pardoned, for we should have said " mule cars." Little, dilapidated, dingy cars,— how queerly they looked

EDUCATION IN DALLAS.

SAN JACINTO SCHOOL

CUMBERLAND HILL SCHOOL.

to our northern eyes, as, in turn, they came jauntingly down the street, each drawn by a pair of lank, diminutive mules, driven by ununiformed drivers who, by the aid of a formidable lash attached to a huge whip-stock, obtained from these " long-eared " animals effective service. These cars, too, are "bob-tail."

By means of these cars, however, notwithstanding their "outs," we visit many interesting interior sections of the city, and also penetrate into its rural retreats. Our rides into the suburban districts show to us a broad expanse of territory, but sparsely occupied, representing residences and varied industries. Cotton fields, with their blooms, and with their white woolly heads, interspersing here and there, gives fine effect to the beauty of the out-lying country. One of the more noted of the industries visited was " Munger's Cotton Gin." This, although not a new device, was of itself decidedly new, comprehending the old-fashioned cotton gin in its accomplishment, but so improved and amplified as to be a new invention of extensive utility and great practicability. Without attempting a description of its mechanism, it is of interest to say that this machine is located in a building erected expressly for it, to which is attached a roofed-in driveway. A wagon loaded with the raw product of cotton, right from the cotton field, drawn to this building and under its driveway, has lowered into it an immense tube connected direct with this cotton gin. By means of steam power the machinery is operated, and through the tube the load of cotton is drawn up and into the cotton gin. This

COTTON PICKING IN TEXAS.
START FOR DINNER.

improved machine separates the cotton seed from the cotton heads, picking it all apart, and then passes the cotton on into a hydraulic compress of tremendous power, there it is made into a cotton bale, covered, strapped; and prepared ready to forward to the cotton mill. Thus from the loaded wagon direct from the field, this wonderful machine takes the cotton and holds it until it is a cotton bale ready for shipment. It is an invention promising great advantage to this southern industry, and was the result of many years of patient study and labor on the part of its inventor.

A visit to the stock-yards and meat-packing establishments, on the outskirts of the city was very interesting, and revealed to us the operation of this comparatively new enterprise. At these stock-yards may be seen fine specimens of the Texan steer, with long, beautifully curved and wide spreading horns. These horns from the slaughtered cattle are utilized in different ways. Some of them, polished to a high degree, are wrought in exquisite designs into chairs, rockers, stools, hat-trees, and other household devices of great beauty.

A profound study in this city, as indeed throughout the south, is the Negro population, or, as we would say at home, the colored people. But the Negroes of the south and the colored people of the north, while belonging to the same race, are essentially two different classes. The colored problem of the south is a serious one, and the future of this race in this section will be interestingly watched by the entire country. With the liberties

BY JINGO!

accorded to the blacks of the north, the unlimited school privileges extended to them, the unrestricted freedom of use of all public conveyances, in fact, in all public matters, enjoying equal rights with the whites, they have thus had bestowed upon them social and educational advantages which have elevated them to a high plane. Not so with the Negroes of the south, whose environment, measured from any standpoint, has been directly opposite. Originally servitors of toil, knowing only masters who owned them as other chattels of barter and sale, without educational opportunities, these sable children of the south have been trained to a far different life. Emancipation liberated them from an involuntary servitude, but it did not remove the social barriers which for years have isolated and ostricised these people. Largely due to these humiliating and separating circumstances, the southern Negro early learned to disregard honor, chastity, and the common rights of others, and thus lapsed into a laxity of good manners, and an almost utter disregard of morals,—a nearly total disrespect for person and property has resulted.

A great change, however, in the social condition of these southern blacks has been gradually growing during the past quarter of a century, or a little more, due chiefly to educational advantages which have been extended to them. They are, notwithstanding this satisfactory fact, still an illiterate people, taken as a whole, relegated to a life by themselves, and it will be many years yet before they will attain to a realization of the high type of social existence enjoyed by the more fortunate colored people of the north.

Whatever else may be said of the southern Negroes, it is true that they are kind-hearted, susceptible to sympathy, appreciate kindness, and a pleasant word addressed to them is "like apples of gold in pictures of silver," and elicits a ready response. In their lives, their manners, their actions, they are, in an extreme sense, a peculiar people, ludicrous and marvellous. They are pathetic, enthusiastic, fervent, and naturally religious.

BAPTIST CHURCH, DALLAS.

Notice of "colored camp-meeting" services, conducted by "Sin-Killer Griffin," coming to our attention by distributed hand-bills, we determined on a visit to the tent where these services were held. Proceeding thither on Sunday evening, we found, under a wide spreading canopy, a large open-air auditorium, with seats rudely constructed of hard, coarse, unplaned planks. There was a goodly assemblage of "de cullud folks," together with quite a sprinkling of whites, or rather a company of whites seated by themselves,— this latter class, as was plainly evident, present from curiosity and to watch the singular proceedings. Occupying an elevated platform was a muscular, black as ebony, burly Negro preacher, weighing upwards of two hundred pounds, and who titled himself "Sin-Killer Griffin." Born in slavery, as he told us, he was illiterate and individually distinctive, yet was, nevertheless, well versed in the Scriptures, and had a ready flow of speech. In a circle back of him was a company of about twenty Negroes of both sexes, of varying shades, who, to the accompaniment of a small cabinet organ which had seen better days, rendered "sacred songs" unique, and which were, unquestionably, of pure southern plantation character. As they sang, every muscle of their bodies, and each part of their physical organism, seemed to move in unison with their singing, while with their feet they made the platform on which they sat tremble as they "beat out" the time. The composition of these "jubilee hymns" was indisputably original, and one could hardly refrain from forgetting the intended sacredness of the occasion as these remarkable exercises were rendered. As sample of the words sung, the following is an illustration:

Roll on the Gospel Chariot.

Roll on the Gospel chariot and crush out Satan's plans,
The Savior calls, " come view my wounds, my feet, and bleeding hands;
For you I bore the cruel cross, for you the death and shame,
For you the painful crown of thorns, for you the triumph came."

Chorus.— Get on the Gospel chariot, yes get on board to-night,
  Bells are ringing, train is waiting, 'twill soon be out of sight.
  O, get on the Gospel chariot, yes get on board to-night,
  Bells are ringing, train is waiting, 'twill soon be out of sight.

Roll on the Gospel chariot, the gates are open wide,
Come weary, doubting sinner, come, for you the Savior died;
With bated breath the angels wait, all heaven bids you come,
They open wide the golden gate, here's pardon, rest, and home.

Chorus.— Roll on the Gospel chariot, etc.

Roll on the Gospel chariot, and call the wand'rers in,
The Savior died and rose again to save a world from sin;
Come sing the old, old story, and make the anthems ring,
We'll join the throng, and chant the song of triumph to our king.

Chorus.— Roll on the Gospel chariot, etc.

Over and over again, twenty or thirty times, was this chorus sung and resung, to the interspersed verses repeated, the whole life of the singers being engulfed in the sentiment of the " hymn." To show the variety and unlikeness of these melodies, in finish and in thought, we give another sample. The verses of this one was sung as a solo, or rather, in a cracked voice, howled, by a sable so-called "jubilee singer," and ran as follows:

Traveling Pilgrim Song.

(*Song Composed by R. H. Hawkin. Containing Bible Proofs.*)

   Chorus. Oh, you must be born again,
              Oh, you must be born again.

If you had a hundred sheep and one of them should go astray, would you leave the ninety and nine, go into the valley and search until you find him, and when you find him put him on your shoulder, bring him back to the fold again and help me to rejoice? I done found the sheep which was lost.

Chorus.—

There was another man in the city of Babylon whose name was Nebuchadnezzar, taken those three little Hebrew boys, Shadrach, Meshach and Abednego, and they cast them into the fire, and the King could not rest all night long. The King came down right early in the morning and looked into the burning furnace. Look a-here King, did'nt we cast in three. The King said yes. We cast in three but behold I see four walking in the fire and the fourth one looks like the Son of Man. I heard them children begin to sing, I know I've been redeemed.

Chorus.—

Nicodemus being King Ruler of the Jews and the same came to him by night, saying Rabbi, we know thou art a Teacher come from God, no man can do the miracles that thou does except God be with him. Lord God said unto Nicodemus except a man be born again he can't enter into the kingdom of Heaven, and won't that be a time.

Chorus.—

Well, I tell you how that hypocrit do go ride about the neighborhood, and talk about you, talk about Sally, talk about Jane, sure tell Jane don't you call my name, under these things of God I will trust. I would tell her so myself, but I am afraid I will make a fuss, help me to read on down.

Chorus.—

Read the scripture I am told, about the garment that Achan stole, he hid it in the thistles, the thorns and the hedges down in the camp, beneath the golden wedge. I got my stickel steeple and my staff. Moses ground up the golden calf and put it into the water, turn bitter as gall. The children of Israel couldn't drink it at all. Help me to read on down.

Chorus.—

And the preaching! Such we never heard before! To us there was " nothing like it in the heavens above, in the earth beneath, or in the waters under the earth." The preacher, in all the enthusiastic effectiveness characteristic of his race, discoursed to his hearers,— now in serious vein, now in comical imagery, and again in the most pathetic monotone,— producing pronounced results on many of these impetuous, susceptible black attendants, throwing them into hysterical convulsions, and in some instances causing them to become so rigidly stiff as to require their being carried from the scene to the greensward of the adjoining lot, leaving them there to " come to " in time to seek home before midnight. And thus these strange exercises went on, and we were involuntarily impelled to attend on a second occasion. Grotesque, laughable, and yet, withal, sacredly pathetic, these " colored camp-meeting" services, in this far-away southwestern city, gave us an experience as novel as it was unfamiliar to us.

Much more did we observe and enjoy in Dallas. From arrival to departure we were accorded an open, free, genuine, southern hospitality; we found the people affable, gracious and generous, and alert to make every moment of our sojourn agreeable. And so the days of our "week in Dallas" passed all too quickly, and brimful of delightful experiences, as they were, they will remain fragrant in memory while reason lasts. The week gone, our thoughts, instinctively, turn to home, loved ones, business and our daily haunts; we say farewell, and quit these varied scenes which have furnished to us naught but pleasure and instruction.

Departing from Dallas, we proceed homeward over the same route by which we came, except the side trip to Hot Springs. The ever dissolving views of nature, spread out like a grand panorama, evidencing the creative power of the Supreme Father, and showing the genius and mechanical skill of man, are as entertaining to us in rotrospect as they were enchanting to us on our outward trip. Each connecting railroad by which we ride is of the best in the great railway system of the Republic, and the courtesies and attentions of the officials are constant and unreserved. Our trip was arranged by Mr. Charles A. Florence, the New England Agent of the Illinois Central railroad, who accompanied us from Boston to St. Louis. His personal presence added, in no small degree, to the pleasure of the journey, and he was untiringly vigilant in catering to our individual comfort.

With these delightful experiences, narrated in this descriptive outline of our journey, we venture the assertion that, for pleasure, comfort, and unsurpassed natural scenery, there is no better route or system of connecting railways than those by which we travelled, for the tourist who makes a long or

A BRIEF TRIP TO THE SOUTHWEST.

www.ingramcontent.com/pod-product-compliance
Lightning Source LLC
Chambersburg PA
CBHW030345170426
43202CB00010B/1257